The Tiny Guide to Huge Success

100 Biz Boosting Hot Tips to Ignite YOUR Performing Career

Jeri Goldstein

PERFORMING BIZ

Original Cover Design: Carole Ehrlich
Book Design: Margaret Smith

Published and distributed by:
Performingbiz, LLC
Delray Beach, FL 33484
jg@performingbiz.com
https://performingbiz.com

*To the artists I have booked and managed in the past,
thank you for starting me on this journey.*

*To my recent and current consulting clients,
thank you for your commitment
and constant inspiration.*

*To the artists already benefiting from
Biz Booster Hot Tips,
thank you for providing the spark
to ignite my creativity.*

*To my industry friends and colleagues,
thank you for your continued work
in the service of the performing arts.*

STOP!

Please Log On for My
Important Welcome Message
https://performingbiz.com/4u2

Other Books By Jeri Goldstein

How To Be Your Own Booking Agent
The Musician's & Performing Artist's Guide
To Successful Touring

The Tiny Guide to Huge Success
100 Biz Boosting Hot Tips to
Ignite Your Performing Career—Volume 1
(Paperback, Kindle, E-Reader, PDF)

Table of Contents

Foreword

In October 1999 I officially entered into the world of independent music, publishing the first edition of a music directory called the *Indie Bible*. Around that same period (the Neolithic Age of the Internet), music websites in the hundreds, and soon thousands, began to appear online. Most didn't survive for long, but many did, and became cornerstones of the massive technological explosion of art and sound, that is today's Independent Music Industry.

In 1999 CD Baby had recently started up. Derek Sivers was running it out of his house in Woodstock, New York. Live365 introduced a new Internet radio technology-one that paved the way for today's Internet radio stations and podcasts, which number in the tens of thousands. Panos Panay of Sonicbids was promoting a new promotional tool that he had invented called the Electronic Press Kit (EPK). People thought it was pretty weird, and it was a hard sell at first. The EPK has now become an industry standard. Indie-Music.com was a new haven for unsigned artists, providing education and support, and still remains strong today. The Muse's Muse opened its doors as a resource for struggling songwriters who were trying to find some footing in this new musical explosion. And at a very small music conference I attended in Ottawa, Richard Gotterer, founder of The Orchard, shared his vision to the audience—some crazy ideas he had about people downloading music for free. An action he claimed would change the very face of the music industry.

Another star began to shine at this time. It was a DIY manual by a woman named Jeri Goldstein. The book was called *How to Be Your Own Booking Agent: The Musician's & Performing Artist's Guide to Successful Touring.* It soon became an industry classic.

For fourteen years this award winning book has been among the top selling music and performing arts business books. It is regularly selected by professors teaching music business classes in colleges and universities throughout the United States and Canada. I don't know anyone in the music business that hasn't heard of it.

The important thing to note is that Jeri didn't write this book and then move on to something else. Jeri has continued to educate herself, committing her research to this one particular area. For many years she has been the "brain center" of all things touring and playing live. She is "THE" resource. There is no one on the planet that is as knowledgeable about this area of the music industry.

Jeri lectures, attends conferences and hosts her own educational web-seminars in order to help artists understand what is needed to create a successful live show.

Jeri's new book *The Tiny Guide to Huge Success: 100 Biz Boosting Hot Tips to Ignite Your Performing Career* is a wonderful collection of tips developed through her research and prompted by the thousands of questions she's been asked over the years. As the title indicates, the book consists of 100 tips that cover "every" imaginable area of touring and playing live.

The initial tips in the book are boosters that will help you to build a foundation. These first boosters cover the basics on how to communicate, feel confident, deal with rejection, and other important character-builders that will help ensure, that when the time comes to actually start booking and then performing, you will find success.

It's one of those resources that you'll refer to for years, and will always discover something fresh and new that you had never noticed before.

If you play live at all, the information in this book will exponentially increase your chances of success. It will also enable you to avoid the many dark holes that touring artists continually find themselves falling into.

So here's to the new you . . . up on stage, and making a lasting impression!

David Wimble
January 29, 2012

Introduction

On August 18, 2007, Biz Booster Hot Tips were born. Four years and over 222 Biz Boosters later, listeners, readers, followers and friends have grown in numbers. I've often been asked to put together a collection, easily accessible, available for quick review and reference. Here are 100 of my favorite Biz Boosters, gathered neatly together in Volume 1, created in multiple formats for your listening and/or reading convenience.

My book, *How To Be Your Own Booking Agent,* first published in 1998 along with all the updates and editions over the years, offers a performing artist an in-depth touring and career planning guide. Biz Booster Hot Tips have allowed me to continue providing current strategies week after week to further enhance your career growth.

The Tiny Guide to Huge Success touches upon a variety of topics to help you round out your professionalism. These topics were inspired by questions asked by artists, agents, managers and presenters during the past few years and resulted in the weekly Monday Morning Biz Booster Hot Tip.

Each tip was purposefully brief and meant to be considered and acted upon during the week it was offered, as one step to move your career forward. Now, this collection of 100 Biz Boosting Hot Tips, were specifically selected to help you grow as a well-rounded professional touring artist and entrepreneur.

Take this volume as a "Big Picture" career overview offering a vision of what could be done to reach your career goals and how to do it. Then, take each Biz Booster, one at a time and begin, to ignite your career with solid, easy to implement, strategies. As you move from one Biz Booster to the next, you'll experience new confidence, see your skill level rise, develop deeper relationships with your business contacts and will be able to laser-focus on the priorities and decisions necessary to direct your career.

I've been amazed at the comments sent by Biz Booster fans over the last few years. One artist took one tip and used it to book multiple dates in his area and get press coverage, gig after gig, month after month using Biz Booster #68. Or, another artist increased his income at club dates just by using Biz Booster #56. The success stories keep me writing each week to find new ways to help your career grow.

Whether you are just starting your performing career or you are a tour-savvy road warrior, *The Tiny Guide to Huge Success* may just have a few Biz Boosting Hot Tips to ignite some aspect of your performing career. Dive in, pick a topic, pick a tip and get started. I can't wait to hear your success stories.

Jeri Goldstein
Charlottesville, VA
January 18, 2012

Audience Development

Biz Booster #1
Add More Names to Your Mailing List
Old Tech, New Tech

Have you ever packed up your merchandise table and wondered why more people hadn't signed your mailing list? Stop waiting for them to come to you. If you want to build your fan base you've got to invite them and entice them!

Here's how-Old Tech: Create a post card size form to hand to everyone as they enter or place the cards in the seats before the doors open. On it, ask for all the info you want to collect: name, address, email, age, occupation, and whatever other questions you might want to know, but keep it brief. Invite them to fill out the cards and collect them before the first set is over. Entice them with a drawing which you will hold before the first break, to win a free CD or piece of merchandise.

Here's how-New Tech: This requires some website in-advance set-up. If you use an email service or collect new contacts on your website or on your social network sites, add a few of the suggested bits of information from above to your online form. Make sure that you have set up a free thank-you gift like a download, a newsletter or free report to be accessed once they've signed up. During the first set, invite everyone who's got their smart phones handy, to go to either your website or specify one of your social network sites where you have your sign up form, but only direct them to one particular site. Have them sign up right there. Then you can log into that site and see all the names. Scroll through the recent sign-ups in the last few minutes and randomly select a name. That's your winner for that set or that night.

Now, you've collected names from almost everyone, you've shown your appreciation by giving them something, and you've created interest in the CD and Merchandise Table. Good luck!

Biz Booster #2
Gigs with Big Audiences

Tired of playing for small crowds? Want to build your recognition within a larger marketplace? Want to play in front of hundreds if not thousands? Then it's time to knock on the doors of city hall. Yes, local government departments are a great place to find some big audience gigs.

You know the ones I'm talking about. Ever see the whole community turn out at the local band stand or amphitheater or city park? Who goes to these concerts, the whole town perhaps? Well why aren't you playing on that stage in front of all those people? It is possible you know.

Let's break down the process of getting those gigs. Pay attention to your local papers, the arts paper and the daily paper and look for ads promoting the local events occurring in town. These may be prime spring, summer and fall events. Sometimes there are even winter events like New Years Eve First Night celebrations.

Attend a few if you haven't already and ask the sound guy, "Who is the person who books the talent." They will always know who to direct you to if they are a sound company hired by the city. If they came with the band, then ask the band. You could also go to the city's website and look for links to the concert series, recreation department, Downtown Foundation or just call city hall and ask for the contact.

Find out when they book the next season and if you're really bold, ask if you can open for a show they've already booked this season, just to get your foot in the door. Drop off some promo or email a link to your EPK, website or Facebook Page. They'll probably want to get direct contact information and will want to download your bio, see a video and listen to your music.

There are other types of large-audience events that occur in your county and province, so start looking through the events calendar for events that are not just club listings, but are events like fairs, local festivals, races or even ball games. By looking beyond the regular performance venues you can begin to broaden your recognition within your community and your region.

One final note, just because many of these events may be free to the public, they are events that pay their performers. Don't discount them just because the audience doesn't have to pay. And, don't feel compelled to play for less either. There are budgets for these events and you should start by asking for a realistic fee. Do your budgeting, position yourself appropriately and don't undersell yourself.

By playing for these events, attended by the general population, you have a chance to widen your audience, gain fans that might not ever have sought you out or come to the venues you normally play.

My motto for building an audience has always been, when the fans won't come to you, you go to the fans. If you think of more places where people gather for events and turn them into potential performance opportunities, you will build a larger fan base, sell more CDs and get more people to come to your other gigs.

Biz Booster #3
Focus On Your Audience

I have long been advocating to my clients, that when you gain a deep understanding of who your audience is, you will be able to communicate with them more effectively. By knowing their needs, their wants, their concerns, you can develop the appropriate marketing tools, products and services to match.

What does this mean for you? This one concept of focusing on your audience can affect the quality and quantity of your bookings, your merchandise sales, your media coverage as well as the ultimate success of any of your projects. Wow! That's huge, right!

Now, let's take a look at some of your promo materials, like your bio, your press releases and your website. I'd like you to re-read these and make a list of how many times you use the words, I, we and our and then make a list of how many times you use the words you, your and yours. If the majority of your writing includes I, we and our, then you are not focusing on your audience or various audiences.

What does it mean to focus on your audience? For one thing, it means you must develop a relationship, a deeper understanding of their needs, wants and concerns, so you may interact with them more effectively. And secondly, once you begin to understand their needs, wants and concerns, you can create messages and performances that demonstrate to them that you get them and are creating with their specific needs, wants and concerns in mind.

And what does this do for you? It makes you unique among your peers and it creates trust, respect, empathy and loyalty. These are all things that you will need in order to have a thriving career for many years. Over the long term, it will help you book better gigs, sell more merchandise and get more media coverage.

For now, review your marketing materials and make your lists so that you can begin to serve your audiences more effectively and in turn you will be serving your career.

Biz Booster #4
Create Your Own Niche Market

Are you following the crowd? Are you going after all the same venues that every other act in your market is going after? No wonder you might be finding it hard to get gigs that pay decent fees.

It might just be time to start looking for your own niche market, reduce the competition and increase the number of gigs you do along with the income each gig offers. Ah, but how do you do this?

The first step to remove the competition is to identify your own unique niche market. I'd like you to think about a few things and make some lists.

What are your interests? Perhaps you are interested in certain sports like golf, skiing, baseball, football, tennis or fishing? Maybe you practice Yoga or meditation or you like to cook or visit wineries. Maybe you are a collector. Make a list of your interests and think about what kinds of groups or organizations are also interested in similar things.

Do you have any special affiliations? In this case you might have religious or charitable affiliations. You may also be a member of a political, trade or social organization. These organizations often have meetings and conferences and will often hire entertainment for their meetings. Perhaps your affiliation will give you an in with a like-minded group.

What are you past work experiences? Looking back at any jobs you may have had either while you were performing or even before you began performing, you may discover a great niche market to tap. Draw upon your past work experience to find potential niche markets and call upon old colleagues as a way to gain access to a whole new market.

Making lists of these three areas of your life just might open some new doors to a whole new performance market where you, and you alone, can stand out and be the go-to performer. Reduce your competition and create your own niche market by looking at your life in a whole new way. You just might find a blossoming career.

Booking Psychology

Biz Booster #5
Phone-Phobia: Do You Have It?

Phone-phobia is the fear of making phone calls. Every artist and agent I know loves to receive them, especially when it's a call to book a gig.

What's behind this phobia, why is it so common among artists who book themselves and more importantly, is it affecting you?

I did some research on this phobia because I run into all sorts of artists who hate making calls and a few reasons stood out to me.

Fear of Rejection: Now that is a big one. This one has the potential to make you avoid calling prospective bookers immediately. No one likes to be rejected, right? But, as an artist doing your own booking, it could be even more of a problem because you could feel like your work is being rejected and that hurts.

Uncertain of What to Say: This is another huge obstacle you may be experiencing when attempting to make calls. When that occurs you may come off sounding scattered and unprofessional. This will certainly add to your lack of confidence in an already uncomfortable situation.

Uncomfortable Selling Yourself: Many artists are hesitant to make booking calls because they don't like to sell themselves or "toot their own horn." I've heard this often. They don't like listing their accomplishments in a self-promoting way.

These are just some of the most often talked about reasons that make it hard for self-booking artists to actually pick up the phone and call on their own behalf.

Examine these three reasons and see if any one or all three might be hampering you from making the calls you need to make on your own behalf.

The next few Hot Tips offer some suggestions as to how you might counter these three phobias and help you to find ways to set yourself up for a more positive relationship with booking calls.

I don't care how many mass emails you may send to potential bookers, reality is, that each booking is an individual relationship, requiring you to deal with individuals and unique situations. Until you can become comfortable with the eventual one-to-one relationship-building techniques and use the phone call or strategically written email, your bookings may suffer. And I want to make sure that doesn't happen.

Biz Booster #6
Phone-Phobia Part One:
Counter Your Fear of Rejection

Booking a gig is really a matter of being chosen over the many numbers of other artists vying for the same gig you are. So when making booking calls, there is always that chance that you will not be chosen. And here is where fear of rejection comes into play. If you make the call, you might be rejected or not chosen. If you don't make the call you avoid the whole experience of feeling or being rejected.

We all want to be accepted. We all want to be chosen. It lets us know we are doing something well or right or beautiful.

Now when it comes to creating art or music or performance of any kind, we want to be in demand by an appreciative audience.

So how do you create a situation where your calls for gigs can reduce or remove the possibility of being rejected and increase the opportunities of being chosen?

Make Friendly Calls. This means start with people or contacts that either you already know or who have been referred to you by people you know. It also means starting with calls within a close circle of contacts rather than calling large venues that have little chance of knowing who you are. If you have pockets of fans in multiple markets, start with them to create multiple or mini-home bases of support.

By focusing on known contacts, friends, friends of friends who might help refer you to people in the industry, put together a house concert or recommend you to contacts they know, you reduce the stress of making completely cold-calls.

By starting with known contacts, you practice your pitch, get more comfortable with the calling process and have more of a chance of being received well by the call recipient. This will raise your comfort level and your confidence.

I'm a firm believer that creating a tight circle of connections, close to home-base and expanding outward, builds a strong foundation of fans, venues and media. This creates market demand; at first in a small area and then expands wider and wider. Creating market demand increases the potential of being chosen more often over time and less chances of being rejected.

If being rejected prevents you from picking up the phone to make the calls you need to make to book your gigs, try making these so-called, *friendly calls* first, before attempting to call an unknown contact. You will begin to reduce your fear of rejection and your phone-phobia.

Biz Booster #7
Phone-Phobia Part Two:
Prepare Your Calls

Making booking calls may not be your favorite thing to do, but at some point you just have to get to it. It may just be that when you have the added pressure to get the job done, it might be exactly the wrong time to make the calls. If you jump into a calling session unprepared you may come off scattered and unprofessional. That's not the picture you want to paint of yourself and your act.

To avoid this problem, the best thing you can do is to practice your calls, prepare for them ahead of time. Knowing what you are going to say when you call is only half the picture, the other half, is knowing as much as possible about the venue or contact you are calling.

Preparing for your calls is all about doing a bit of research about the venue, their schedule, their previous presentations and the community in which they present their performances. This approach is different from just sitting down with a long database of potential venue numbers and calling one after another. This approach focuses you on the venues you really want to play and that make sense for you as an artist. This reduces the *numbers* of calls and concentrates your efforts on the *right* calls. By understanding as much as you can about the venue, you are able to really formulate a conversation that includes the call recipient and talk about how you and your act can really fit into their performance schedule.

When you approach a call with research to back you up, a deep understanding of what you have to offer the venue and why it would work in their venue, your call comes across more professionally, more organized and with a sensitivity to the venue's objectives and situation.

The more laser-focused you are with information about your act, what you are trying to achieve, research about the venue and how your act can provide something unique to their schedule, the more comfortable you will be during the call process. The more time you spend preparing for each call, you will be able to turn more calls into gigs, more often.

So the next time you pick up the phone to make a booking call, ask yourself if you are really ready to make this call? Have you done enough research to prepare for this call to make it count? When you pick up the phone to make calls, just to get the job done, you may find yourself less effective. The more prepared you are to make your calls, the more calls you will begin making with confidence, professionalism and greater results.

This week, pick a venue or two and prepare your calls to those venues. Do some research, plan your pitch, practice your call and make your call with confidence. You will then have this phone-phobia under control.

Biz Booster #8
Phone-Phobia Part Three:
Establish Your Value

This final part on conquering your phone phobias, discusses how to establish your value to the person with whom you are speaking to get a gig.

I often hear that artists don't like to, "toot their own horn" and talk about themselves in a positive promotional manner. It's often uncomfortable to talk about yourself and what a great act you are. So why not let others tell your story for you and use their words and not yours?

This is why getting testimonials, media quotes and reviews can be helpful and why it is so important to get these for every gig you do. These words about your act by media, promoters, and fans can help you tell your story while you are speaking to potential buyers.

Let's say the buyer asks you why they should book you over another act. You can pull out your review in the "such and such newspaper" that said, "The band delivers every time, the audience loved them." You can also pull out the testimonial from the presenter and say, "Here's what Presenter x from the performing arts center said about working with us," then recite the testimonial.

This method of, "tooting your own horn," becomes less painful and much more credible. The buyer you are speaking with will be much more moved by the words of another presenter, rather than your own anyway.

Make every effort to get those testimonials and quotes from previous places you've played and try very hard to invite reviewers to your gigs so you can get reviews. This will give you valuable feedback and usable comments to help tell your story or *establish your value* in your markets. It will make it much easier for you to sell yourself when you use the words of others who the buyer will hold in high regard.

This method of promoting yourself on the phone will help conquer the third most often sited phone phobia among artists. I hope it helps you get many more gigs in the future as you dive into making your phone calls to book gigs.

Goals & Planning

Biz Booster #9
A Breakfast of Creative Planning

Have you had your breakfast this morning? Do you start your business day with a cup of Joe and then jump on the phone to book the next tour or jump on the bus to get to the next gig?

Just as food fuels our body to run at its peak, your performing business needs its daily dose of fuel also, in this case, how about a jolt of creative planning!

Why not spend a few minutes brainstorming a list of ten new ideas you can put to use. For example: some new marketing or promotional ideas, song titles, song topics, theme names for tours, ideas for news stories to pitch to the media, some catchy press release titles, some intriguing email subject line ideas, some new types of venues you want to play, some businesses you want to speak with about sponsorships, ideas for the next newsletter, I think you get it.

Be creative and take some time each morning to feed your career with a jolt of creative planning then take action and get to work on them. You'll be amazed at the changes you'll begin to see in your career.

Biz Booster #10
Benefits of a Short Call List

We all have enough on our to-do list to keep us overwhelmed for a long time. Booking calls are necessary, but let's face it, if you look at a list of one hundred calls that need to be made this week, you get overwhelmed and under enthused about picking up the phone. Instead, shorten the list, and I mean really short. How about five calls!

Start the week with five calls on your list. The first thing that happens is you'll probably think, "I can do that, piece of cake!" So you start calling with a sense of having already accomplished the five calls.

The best part is that your enthusiasm will be reflected in your voice and your personality so you'll come across like a winner.

The next great thing to happen is that if you work these five calls with confidence and connect in positive ways with each of the five prospects, you can add another call to the list. Now you are buzzing right along, feeling accomplished and successful in your booking calls for that week.

Begin the week with achievable expectations rather than potentially overwhelming frustrations.

Small Lists = Big Results!

Biz Booster #11
Time Management: *Your* Most Important Job

Ask yourself this question, "What is the most important thing that you do as a performing artist?" If you answered, "create your, music, your theater, your art," then the most important thing that you need to schedule, each and every day, is a time when you can do your most important thing, your art.

What is your prime time of day? When are you most creative or productive at the thing that is most important to you? Now, get out your calendar, day timer, scheduler, phone, whatever tool you use to plan your appointments, and block out time each day to do what is most important to your creative life.

If you don't schedule time in each day to that thing that makes *you* who *you* are as a person and as an artist, then your day will fill with all sorts of distractions and you will ask a question like, "How do you juggle all the parts of your life and have time left to do your art?" First make time for your art, then, the rest will follow.

Biz Booster #12
Time Management:
Short, Focused Time-Blocks

Schedule shorter, focused time-blocks to accomplish more. Do you feel like you never get anything done, always flitting from one thing to another? Do you take pride in the fact that you are great at multi-tasking? Multi-tasking can come in handy doing certain tasks, like cooking, but when you are trying to complete something in your business, it may be less helpful.

Try this. Pick something on this week's to do list. Schedule a time-block of between one to two hours depending on the complexity of what you want to accomplish. Write that block of time in your scheduler.

Using shorter blocks of time, with a beginning and an end gives your day structure. Now, as a creative person, leaving the day without structure, may seem more familiar to you and even more comfortable. By creating time-blocks, there adds a sense of necessity for completion. Once completed, you'll feel good and can move on to the next thing after taking a break. If you are working on a large project, like booking the next tour, then scheduling smaller blocks of time with a shorter call list, will also give you a greater sense of accomplishment.

Now let's talk about focused, uninterrupted time-blocks, no distractions. When you sit down to work, turn off your cell phone or land-line, shut your email program so you won't be tempted to check it when you hear that there's a new email. Just concentrate on the work you want to accomplish and do it until it's done or for as long as you have dedicated the time for it. If it is a larger project, make a note about what you would like to work on next when you continue this work in another time-block. You'll get going again much faster. Studies have shown, that by working in fits and starts, each thing takes about twenty to thirty minutes to get back to where you left off.

When you work in shorter time-blocks, your day will fly by, and you will look back and be amazed at how much you accomplished, while feeling like you hardly worked at all. After each time-block, you can take a well deserved break, go for a walk or have a meal, and not feel like the day is getting away from you with nothing getting done.

Look at your week, give it a try. Send me some stories about your successes.

Biz Booster #13
Planning, Planning, Planning

You may have heard the old adage when referring to real estate that it depends on three things; location, location and location.

According to Michael Gerber, author of *The E-Myth*, when it comes to your business, success depends on three things; planning, planning and planning.

Why do I bring this up now, during this busy holiday season? Mostly because trying to focus on things like bookings and getting gigs is often a frustrating, futile set of activities while everyone else is focused on parties and wrapping up their yearly performance season.

I always look at December as my planning month so that when January comes around I'm in doing mode. Since January is my birthday month, it seems that it is my most productive and energized month of the year, so I want to take full advantage of that energy.

So what's a hard-working performing artist to do when you're not performing at holiday gigs? Plan your next tour, your next project, your next marketing campaign, your next year, your next vacation, your end-of-year tax deductions, your retirement contribution . . . what's that?

I know, sounds like work when it's really time to have some fun. Ah, but that is what being successful at business is all about, plan now so you can have fun in your life and your business.

I know you hate it when all of a sudden it's March and you don't have any gigs scheduled. A little planning now, during this so-called down time, and your March calendar won't have to look so barren and empty. You may not be able to book the gigs right now, but you can begin planning your call lists, creating some marketing ideas or deciding on touring markets.

I've said it many times, that a two-year planning strategy provides you with momentum, driving your bookings and your projects forward. So take a detour while you are out shopping for holiday gifts and get yourself a large erasable wall calendar with all the months visible at a glance. Tack it up in your office so you look at it everyday without fail. Start filling it in with all the big plans you've got set already. Put your vacation on it, the upcoming conferences you plan to attend, your recording dates for the next project, any tour dates you have set and any you want to do. Use some colored erasable markers just for the fun of it. No it's not high tech, it's a low tech, constantly visible reminder to keep you going, keep you planning ahead and adhering to plans already made.

Enjoy the 80% of business that will make yours a success, the planning stages, so that the 20% of actual doing and carrying out those plans are as fruitfully realized as your plans intend.

Biz Booster #14
Plan for Positive Results

Stop disappointment in its tracks. Plan for positive results each time you contact potential venues. Impossible you say? Perhaps not, when you plan appropriately.

How exactly do you do this? I believe it's all a matter of setting your expectations to meet the situation properly.

How many times do you sit down to make booking calls or write booking emails and expect to get the gig on the first call? C'mon, deep down you are all geared up to book that tour in one sitting. I know—I used to be that person, all anxious and filled with confidence, totally believing that I'd get this tour booked in the morning and could rest on my laurels after lunch. What a fantasy!

But what if you tweaked those expectations and set more realistic goals for each call or each email based on how far along your relationship is with that booking person.

Here's an example: Let's say you are contacting someone for the first time. Yes, you are eager to get a booking with that person, but given where you are within the stages of building your relationship with that person, it is more likely you would create a successful encounter by setting your expectations for that first contact at a lower bar.

If, instead of trying to book the gig on the first call, you approach the person with the expectation of simply meeting them, introducing your act and sharing how your act might be a good match for their venue, you would have accomplished a great deal. If you also suggest a time for a second call to further develop your relationship, find out more about their programming, their time frame for booking, which conferences they attend, then they will get a better sense of your desire to develop a deeper relationship with them, rather than simply get a gig and move on. They may then see that you are in it for the long-haul and you are attempting to build a long-term relationship.

With those expectations set for your first and second calls, you have created a pattern for successful connections. Each successive contact then moves the relationship along to a deeper place. When you plan your call strategy with this pattern in mind, you are building relationships that eventually will grow into gigs. Your belief in yourself as a relationship-builder will grow and your ability to have successful and pleasant communications with booking personnel will drive your booking calls.

As you plan each successive time-frame for your calls, your call expectations will more appropriately match the level of your relationship. Over time, you will book more gigs, more often.

Step away from the *"got-to-get-a-gig-right-now"* thought process and begin planning your contacts to build your relationships. Match your expectations for each communication to where you are in your relationship-building process with each booking person. You will get more positive results, more often and be a much more successful representative for your act.

Biz Booster #15
Research Before You Act

A little research goes a long way to saving you time and money. Here are three ideas where a little research before you act can lead to a more successful outcome, time after time.

Check venue websites for direct contact information before sending emails or before placing booking calls. A review of the venue's website can give you great info about the venue's booking schedule, program history, seating capacity, ticket pricing, staging and technical information as well as the booking contact. You may discover that this is the right venue for you or perhaps you're not quite ready for it just yet.

Look for national and regional trade magazines, e-zines and online media to find *your* genre-specific media outlets to enhance your marketing. Become acquainted with their deadlines so you can easily submit material on time even with your busy touring schedule.

Check with local city and county, parks and recreation departments or local government agencies to see what kind of events they sponsor throughout the year. There are tons of great performance opportunities, right in your own region. You may not have to travel as far as you think to get a great paying, audience-building gig.

Before you pick up the phone and start making lots of unnecessary calls, do some research and be prepared. Save yourself some time and give yourself an edge on the competition.

Biz Booster #16
Overwhelmed with To-Do's

I hear it all the time, there's too much to do and not enough time to do it all. How many minutes ago did you say that one? This is especially true when you are managing your own career or running your own business.

When you are overwhelmed by tasks, you are less effective, right? But did you catch the word tasks? That's right, most of the time we are overwhelmed by tasks. This could be a clue to how you are prioritizing where you place *your* attention. Let's make a few lists so we can see this right in front of us.

List 1: What things do you do most days which produce income? These would include, making booking calls, checking back with previously played presenters for future gigs and referrals, making deals for recordings, publishing, opening-act slots, endorsements, sponsorships, recording sessions with other artists, teaching, networking, building relationships, writing, composing, rehearsing or practicing and perhaps most important-strategically planning for your creative and business future. Please add anything to this list that is unique to you.

List 2: What are the things that you do to support all of your income producing activities? These would be activities such as maintaining mailings lists, researching new gig opportunities, bookkeeping, marketing and promotions, mailing contracts, CDs, merchandise and marketing materials, website creation and maintenance, making travel arrangements, advancing your gigs, maintaining your instruments, gear, touring vehicles and other equipment.

Are you seeing a pattern here? Can some or most of the things on **List 2** be handed off to someone else, like someone you hire part-time? Perhaps when you remove some of these support tasks from the income producing tasks, you create more space for the items on **List 1** that, for now, are the things on which *you* need to be focusing. If you have an agent booking your gigs, then you may be able to remove those items from **List 1**. If you don't have an agent, then those items are crucial to your livelihood. Once you remove the support items though, you can concentrate on those items that move your career forward and increase your income.

These two lists can help you reframe your priorities and reorganize your time so that your time is spent doing the most important things to build your career. It is also much easier to use List 2 to help you create a job description or multiple job descriptions and find some help. This help might be in the form of a person working part time on some of these items and perhaps outsourcing some of the tasks, such as website development and maintenance or mailing list maintenance or start using an online mailing list service if you don't already. When there are tools available to automate certain tasks, find them and incorporate them.

Biz Booster #17
Working in a Bad Economy—Part One

Budget cuts, cancellations, gas price fluctuations, we are all feeling the effects of the current economy. So what's a performer to do?

It's time to get creative. Traditional bookings at clubs, concert halls and festivals are becoming even tougher as presenting organization budgets are pushed to their limits. As a performing artist you need to do two things first:

Examine your performance possibilities: Sure you have your stage show, but what else can you do? Have you developed any workshops or master-classes that can be offered at colleges or in lower grade schools? Can you create a concert/lecture that can be offered to organizations in and around your region and beyond? Do you teach lessons of some sort? Can you take those lessons and turn them into something that can be video taped and put online to be sold on your website, expanding your reach into the broader Internet community? Dig deep—what else can you do that uses and perhaps stretches your talents to their full potential creating multiple streams of income?

Use your mailing list more intentionally: You have a gold mine of connections on your mailing lists. Locked in that treasure chest are people who have already made a commitment to you and your art. Do you know who is on your list? Have you reached out to them for potential house concerts or other events through their businesses or organizations?

Let's talk house concerts for a minute. Here you have a situation where one person doesn't have to come up with a fee in most cases. Your fee can be spread out among neighbors and friends looking for some entertainment outlet that will not cost them the same kind of big bucks that a concert venue may cost.

People are looking for unique, cozy environments where they can gather comfortably, not travel far and get together with friends and neighbors. Tap into your mailing list and ask those fans to host one of these unique gatherings in their home.

Start by going through your lists and identify some of your biggest fans, family members and friends and email or call them directly.

If you have never performed at a house concert, you might consider checking out Concerts in Your Home (http://www.concertsinyourhome.com) for some valuable tips and resources. And, if you've only performed at established house concert series, then it's time to take a lesson from history when artists found their patrons among their followers and performed in their parlors.

Look to your lists of fans and friends. There you may find some eager supporters that may offer a new mode of building your audience during these challenging economic times.

Biz Booster #18
Working in a Bad Economy—Part Two

We've talked about using your mailing list more intentionally. Now I want to focus on how to use social network sites where you've established a following.

If you worked your sites and have built a fan base, then it is time to begin using those networks to, well, network.

Let's do five things. This may require a little time spent getting to know more about your friends and fans. As lovely as it is to see tons of friends' pictures on your page, if you are not actively analyzing who those friends are, you can't use them to build your audience.

So here are five things you can begin doing:

1. Review your friends or Facebook or other social network site contacts to discover where they are from.

2. Send a blast or email from the social network site to those fans and directly invite them to share information with you about their town's performing opportunities.

3. If they are another band or performer, create a specific message asking them about gigs in their area, but even better, ask about swapping gigs so they can open for you and you can open for them. (For more about swapping gigs, check out my article, "Co-Operative Audience Swaps to Break Into New Markets"(https://performingbiz.com/co-operative-audience-swaps-break-new-markets).

4. If they are a fan and not a performer, then ask them for suggestions of places, where they like to go for live performances. Give them some incentive to write back, like a free download of a song, two free tickets to the show booked in their town, you get the idea.

5. And, if you really want to test the fan base, ask if they would like to host a house concert or if they have any connections to a local business, organization, college or school where they could help line something up for you. Again, some incentive would be great here as well. Now don't forget to offer a special invitation for them to visit your main website to find out more about you, sign your regular mailing list or dare I say it, buy something.

Any time you can make your communications inviting, specific and rewarding, then, you are using your contacts more intentionally and booking potential gigs outside the normal mainstream channels.

Making Career-Building Decisions: Remove Your Emotions

How many times a day do you have to make a decision that might impact your career, or even, your life?

What factors do you use to help you make your final decision? Most people are influenced by their emotional response to any given situation. Heck, that's what advertisers count on as do car sales people, real estate agents—you've been there. You remember, "So what color car do you see yourself driving." Emotional, you bet!

When it comes to your career, choosing to take a gig or bring a three piece band instead of the duo, whether to fly or drive or accept the record deal or remain independent, you need to consider the facts and remove your emotions as much as possible.

The fact is that if you follow the money—do the numbers—your decisions will become much easier. You'll either chose one over the other based on concrete numbers that tell you, "You will lose money if you do this." But at least you know that, going into it, especially when other peripheral factors make the deal worth more than the money alone.

Here are six helpful things to consider when making career decisions, especially when it comes to booking your gigs:

1. Work with a budget for each gig or each tour.
2. Include all of your expenses before deciding on the gig fee.

GOALS & PLANNING   25

3. Negotiate any necessary contracts with side band members including per diems and their expenses before quoting gig fees, then include those costs in your budget.
4. Amortize your expenses over the number of dates you intend to tour so you may quote appropriate fees.
5. Ask the booking person about potential travel, housing and meal provisions to help defray your budget expenses. Sometimes they have hotel deals or provide you with meals or a meal allowance. If you don't ask, they may not offer.
6. Ask each booking person about the scope of their publicity opportunities during negotiations, what they will do or have access to so you may include those peripheral benefits in your fee quotes. That will influence what will be acceptable and what won't.

When you begin to think through your decisions with hard cold numbers in front of you, you simply make better decisions.

Biz Booster #20
Tour Planning Strategies:
Take the Guesswork Out of
Where & When to Tour—Part One

This is big world with so many performance opportunities to choose from, it can be quite overwhelming. This is such a huge topic and that I've created a full twelve-hour online course to cover it in-depth, Booking & Touring Success Strategies & Secrets
(Booking & Touring Success Strategies & Secrets
https://performingbiz.com/booking-online-course).

But, we have to start somewhere, and the best place to start is in a place that allows you to incur the least costs to play the date. Start from your central location—your home-base town, city, state, region and work your way out from the center. My articles on "Developing Your

Home Base of Support to Build National Success—Parts 1 and 2" will give you even more insights. (https://performingbiz.com/developing-home-base-support-build-national-success-part-1 and https://performingbiz.com/developing-home-base-support-build-national-success-part-2)

If you study most popular bands from The Beatles, Huey Lewis and the News, Hootie and the Blowfish, Bruce Springsteen, Ani DiFranco and The Dave Matthews Band, you will find that they all first developed a loyal home base of support and then moved out in concentric circles to gain regional recognition.

This is not just a recent phenomenon. Look back to the classical artists like Mozart and Beethoven, each finding a patron in one city and then building their reputations from there.

If you haven't created a loyal fan base right in your own home town, you may be missing great opportunities to build a solid foundation from which to expand. It is here at the home-front where you can gain loyal media supporters, local business support and fans who will tell their friends in the next town to see you or who will follow you to other local gigs when you are close to home. This cuts your travel costs, your lodging expenses and is the least disruptive to your daily life as you grow your audience and your reputation.

If you think there are no places to play in your home town, look beyond the regular concert halls and clubs to local businesses and organizations, city government departments like parks and recreation, wineries, museums, libraries, schools and universities.

And if there still is a lack in your town, find a place that you can call your home-base, even if it's half a country away, as long as you have a commitment to be there often and have begun to develop some following.

When you build out from a central point, you give your fans a chance to keep up with you and spread the word. You give yourself a chance to build your tours upon the successes of the last dates and can return often to nurture your audience and build demand in your area. This is much easier to do when your travel costs are low. As demand in one area builds, so does your leverage with those booking you and you begin to get higher fees, higher ticket prices and eventually better gigs.

Biz Booster #21
Tour Planning Strategies:
Take the Guesswork Out of
Where & When to Tour—Part Two

Let's talk about how to strategically use an anchor date. An anchor date is a date that usually pays a good enough fee to stand alone, set out into the future, which you can surround with other dates and create a tour. These dates can be useful when you are trying to open a new market.

Here are four scenarios that you can use as anchor dates upon which to build a tour.

1. You're getting great radio airplay in a certain town, so you use that to leverage a gig at a good venue in the market. Then you build your tour around that venue.
2. You are going to attend a conference next year, so you use the conference as the anchor date and get gigs *en route* to and from the conference.
3. You are gong to attend a personal event or family gathering, so you can use those dates as an anchor date to build a tour near the gathering and expand or open a new market.
4. You get an offer from a good venue in a new market. Book surrounding dates that get you to and from the venue to create your tour.

When you start with an anchor date, take a close look at the finances or reasons for doing the date before you confirm or issue a contract. With scenario number 4, make sure the anchor date is paying enough money to make it worth doing as a stand alone or a "run-out" in case you don't book enough support dates to create the tour you were hoping for.

Biz Booster #22
How to Prioritize

How do you choose where to put your attention? What are your most important items to do?

Rather than looking at this as the items on your task list that are screaming for your attention, let's reframe how you consider where you place your attention, your time and your energy. Instead of prioritizing tasks, let's look at prioritizing projects and opportunities that will move your career forward.

Use these ten steps to evaluate your options when you consider your priorities.

1. How will this opportunity influence my income?
2. Am I able to act on this right now? If not, when?
3. What do I need to have in place already, before I can act on this?
4. What financial investment will I need to make in order to act on this?
5. What kind of support team do I need to have in place in order to act on this?
6. Do I have the time, energy, desire and commitment to take this on?
7. How much time do I need to complete this project?
8. Is now, the best time to do this?
9. What are the potential results I might gain from this?
10. Are the potential results worth the investment?

If you review every project, every plan to book a new tour, every recording project with this ten-step process, you will become better at prioritizing for the growth of your business instead of simply filling your day with tasks.

Biz Booster #23
Marinating or Procrastinating

Sometimes I get a great idea and mull it over in my mind for a long time. I work on various aspects of the idea, research it, turn it inside out and upside down, sometimes for months before I actually take action and move it from my mind to make it a reality.

That is what I call "**Marinating.**"

Some projects just need time to gel. They need time to come together so that you can actually take action. Some projects need that *marinating* time before you feel comfortable or ready to work on them in a physical sense, like actually recording it or writing it down. I believe that those projects tend to be better once they've been *marinating* for a while, just like a good cut of meat, before being grilled.

Then there are those projects or jobs or tasks that are ready to be acted upon, they really are screaming out to you to get started, and you just don't. You know you have all the tools at hand, you've done the research, you've got the lists right there in front of you, but you just wait. Wait for what? Days fly by, weeks pass, something comes up, so naturally you can't start it now. A month passes and now it just seems like you've missed your window of opportunity, best wait until next year.

That is "**Procrastinating.**"

Can you see yourself in these two scenarios? Does one ring more true for you? I wonder, which one, hmm?

Once you recognize which scenario best fits you,

think about what kind of tasks or projects fit in each. Think about what you need to do to move from *marinating* to taking action on those ideas or projects.

And if you have some things in your *procrastination* list, think about what is preventing you from moving forward on those? What is stopping you from just doing it, whatever it is? Ask yourself why you are putting these obstacles in your way and preventing the success of this project or better yet, your success! If you just started doing it, what would happen?

These might be a great bunch of questions to work on during the holiday season, so that you can begin your new year free from constraints and ready to get down to it.

Biz Booster #24
Planning Tours Around Band Members

How do you plan your tours with enough time to keep your band members from taking other gigs?

We have a number of challenges to deal with here. If you are not working steadily enough to keep your band members exclusively working with you, then you'll certainly need to give them the opportunity to get work when they are able.

Here are a few options to help you with tour planning as well as keep everyone working.

Plan two years in advance. This tour planning strategy helps get things on the calendar far in advance so that anchor dates and dates surrounding those anchor dates can be filled in many months ahead of the actual tour. This can give the band members more advance notice of the work you have in store for them, so they can make commitments to you further in advance.

Design your touring patterns for specific months of the year to be in specific areas or regions of your world. This allows you to strategically look for anchor dates in those target areas and provides you with a sense of urgency and date specificity when speaking with bookers. As you plan further in advance, you relieve yourself of those last minute bookings because as you build your tours in the specific areas, your bookings gain a momentum as you leverage one booking to get another in the area.

Share your tour plans with your band members early in the process so they have your two-year planning schedule on their schedule. They can then alert you to conflicts they may have right from the start. This gives you ample opportunity to find a stand-in for those dates or time-frames. By keeping your band members informed of your booking progress, you both have plenty of time to make alternate arrangements when necessary.

Make a commitment to your band members if you want them to make a commitment to you. Perhaps you need to make a commitment to them that your tour dates will be in place no later than one month prior to the beginning of the tour. If enough dates are contracted by thirty days out for them to commit to the entire tour time, then even when a few days are open, they'll remain committed to the tour. You'll have to have a discussion with your band members to negotiate the magic number of dates that would be sufficient enough for them to make that commitment to you. This also will add an additional sense of responsibility on your part as the booker and perhaps spur you on to get your gigs booked sooner.

With the two-year planning strategy, even if there is a stray open date late in the tour-building process, there ought to be enough surrounding dates booked in the tour to offset a night off, so that band members won't need to jump ship. As you become more proficient at the two-year planning strategy, you'll find your band members will be more committed to your group and look for fewer gigs with other bands since your bookings are more regular.

Biz Booster #25
Best Time to Call to Book Colleges

You called the venue and they were already booked. How many times have you had that happen? Wouldn't it be great to know the best times to call to at least have a fighting chance of getting booked? The next four Biz Booster Hot Tips will help you become familiar with the best times to call a variety of venue types.

Let's start with college gigs, concerts and coffee houses, the gigs put on by the student activities office. Yes, you heard correctly, Student Activities, which means you'll be dealing with student committees.

Booking gigs through the student activities office is best done at their regional and national conferences put on by two organizations in the U.S and one in Canada: NACA—National Association for Campus Activities (http://naca.org), APCA—Association for the Promotion of Campus Activities at (http://apca.com) and COCA—Canadian Organization of Campus Activities (http://coca.org) in Canada.

These sites offer all the showcase and conference deadlines and dates. If you want to play the college circuit then you really do need to check out these organizations. If you play regionally, then each of these organizations offers regional conferences in your area of the U.S. or Canada.

As you will see from these websites, regional conferences occur late summer and throughout the fall. The national conferences occur mid-winter in February and March for the U.S. and in June for Canada. This tells you that students attending these regional conferences are booking for either the next semester or the next year, so we are talking six to twelve months ahead.

If you want to get to the student committee that does the booking, it really is best to meet them at the conference.

Try to get a showcase slot and get a booking while they still have money in the concert budget. Getting to meet the students at the conference gives you a much better chance of reaching them later on when you try to follow up to finalize a gig.

Once you know when these conferences occur, you're able to time your calls to follow up after the conference. This is when they are really committed to finalizing their concert schedule for the next one or two semesters. Oh, and while at the conference, try really hard to meet the student advisor or head of the student activities department, since they are the ones who sign the actual contracts. You want to know them and get them on your side in case it becomes harder to reach the students.

Even if you don't attend any of the conferences, know their conference time schedule so you can time your calls and send your materials during the period right after the conference. That's when they have the money and when they are focused on booking the events they'll be offering their student body.

So, if you want to play colleges, these organizations offer you the best route to college gigs that pay much more than many other types of gigs. Their conferences will help direct you to the right time to make your calls.

Biz Booster #26
Best Time to Call to Book
Performing Arts Centers

Since we recently talked about calling college campus activities for gigs, let's pick up on the college campus, but focus on college Performing Arts Centers. These venues are almost always a completely separate entity from the student activities office and are run most often through the theater or performing arts department. They are also booked by a staff member rather than a student committee.

The programming director will attend a series of completely different booking conferences than the student activities director. APAP—The Association of Performing Arts Presenters (http://www.artspresenters.org) hosts their main booking conference in New York City in mid-January. Along with the main conference there are regional conferences held around the US beginning in mid-August and running through mid-October. And in Canada, CAPACOA—Canadian Arts Presenting Association (http://www.capacoa.ca) has their conference in January.

Both Performing Arts Centers on and off campus attend these conferences. They book theater, dance, opera, family events and popular performers in music and comedy. They tend not to book large rock shows, leaving those concerts to the student activities office.

If you perform in these venues, then you are dealing with the programming director and you'll likely be competing with major booking agencies. But if you want to have any chance of getting gigs at these venues, you must plan at least eighteen to twenty-four months ahead because that's what they are planning for by attending these conferences. They do most of their decision-making from October through December and leave a little room for booking from the conferences in January if they attend.

Again, you need to follow this schedule in order to be taken seriously. If you don't plan on attending any of the booking conferences, then plan your calls right after the conference in your region. This is one of the reasons I urge you to plan at least two years in advance.

Planning to attend any one of these conferences takes long-range planning. If you haven't looked into attending the conference this year, I urge you to simply check each conference website and get a sense of what is offered, the deadlines required and the costs. If this is something that makes sense for you, plan for next year. If you wanted to attend the conference this year, go to get a feel for the event and do not try to showcase or exhibit. This way you'll be much better prepared for next year.

This year, simply note the conference dates and plan any calls or materials to be sent after the conference is over. Wait a few days or a week after their conference to call or email, so the presenters have a chance to catch up and recuperate from the conference. You'll get a much better reception.

With a little research about the performing arts center conferences in your region, when you call you will at least demonstrate your professionalism and be more in step with their booking schedule.

Biz Booster #27
Best Time to Call to Book Clubs

Whereas performing arts centers plan their performance schedule nearly two years out, clubs are more likely to be filling their calendars four to six to eight weeks prior to the play-date. This can be great for filling in last minute gigs or it can be incredibly frustrating if you are planning your tours farther ahead.

Your best time for calling a club is as soon as you know you are planning a tour in their market. Try to get them to place a hold on your desired date. Then it's a matter of you getting back with them to check on that date and whether they are ready to firm it up.

You want to check with each club to see when they finalize their monthly calendar or prepare any strip-ads or monthly promotions. This will give you a clue as to where the booker is in the planning for that month or the next or however far ahead they are actually firming up dates. Once you know the deadline for the booker to have their marketing ready, then you can be more certain of calling prior to that deadline.

As bookers fill their dates, they look for hot tours that may have just announced their schedules. If they can book a hot act when they are coming through, they would be anxious to do that and bump any holds on their calendar. This is why it is so important for you to keep checking back with the booker, making sure they are still holding your desired date. If a larger act is vying for your date, then by keeping in touch with the booker, you might be able to score an opening slot.

If you play clubs, get in touch as soon as you begin planning the tour. Once they know you are going to be in the area, there is more potential for finding a good date that works for you both, placing a hold on a possible date or being considered for an opening slot. Once you are in contact with the club, you can also ask them for other referrals to clubs in the area that would be far enough away to not interfere with their date, but close enough to help build your regional following. These extra potential gigs could help solidify your tour in case the desired venue isn't able to confirm their date.

Unlike performing arts centers or colleges, club dates are more of an ongoing process. Your tour schedule, your tour routing and the club's monthly calendar will be the determining factors suggesting the proper time frames to begin your calls.

Biz Booster #28
Best Time to Call to Book Festivals

Let's talk about the best times to call for festival bookings. I'd also like to share a great booking strategy with you to get two bookings for two years at one festival.

Festivals are an interesting phenomenon. In most cases the artistic director works throughout the year to plan a one-time event. They may attend any number of varieties of booking and performance conferences and other festivals to round out their performance programming depending on the type of festival they book.

One thing is certain, many festival directors are thinking ahead to the next year, even while the current festival is happening. They are considering which acts are working, which workshops are drawing good crowds to the stage and how artists are interacting with one another in multi-performer events.

Never call a festival two months before the current year's festival. They are in prep-mode and there schedule is already being advertised. Avoid calling during the month after the festival is over as they will be in wrap-up mode, or taking a well deserved break.

As soon as you identify a particular festival that you believe would be a good fit for your act, begin making introductions two months after the festival has ended. They will probably begin thinking about new ideas for programming around that time. They will be planning to attend conferences that occur during the year to see new acts. You might want to ask the festival staff which conferences the artistic director attends.

Your calls and your marketing materials must reflect your understanding of how your act can help the festival director provide something interesting for their audience. If this is your first time at a festival, impress them by suggesting they try you out in a daytime time-slot or a side stage to see how your act would work with their audience. If all goes well, try to get them to agree to have you back the next year in a more prime-time slot on a better stage for a better price.

Festivals have many performers competing for slots along with the artists the festival directors are seeking out. You may need to allow a few years of relationship-building to evolve before you actually get on the bill.

Biz Booster #29
Best Time to Call to
Book Elementary Schools

Summer ends all too quickly and for some areas of the country, kids are back in school by mid-August as in my county in Virginia.

Booking elementary school gigs requires that your timing flow in step with the school year. This means plenty of planning for bookings at least a semester ahead. One thing you learn when performing at elementary schools is that when school is out, there is usually no one around to work with on your future gigs. So, your timing to reach the right personnel at the schools needs to be focused on when they are planning their cultural programming.

Let's go semester by semester. If you want gigs for the fall, you need to plan your calls during April and May before school gets out for the summer. You may call or send your promotions in early September or late August depending on when your school system gets back from summer vacation to get late fall and winter gigs.

Plan on late fall calls beginning in November to book gigs in spring if you haven't already scheduled them from your early fall calls.

Now who exactly do you call? If you've been at this for some time, you probably know the right individuals for your school systems. My very first call would be to the state or provincial Arts Council. They are very likely to have a database of schools who receive grants for school programming and residencies along with appropriate contacts. Once that's done you might then try to call the district office to find out whether they have an arts program coordinator for the district. They may schedule events for the entire system or sponsor a showcase for artists. After that, I'd target specific schools and their principals to find out whether they work with someone specific in their school, like the music teacher or a specific Parent Teacher Organization or Association—PTO or PTA.

Your goal for these initial calls would be to find out exactly who is doing the cultural programming, when they do their booking for the semester or the year and whether they attend any conferences or showcases so you can get involved and make your next year's bookings even easier.

Biz Booster #30
Momentum Motivation

Are you stuck! Does if feel like you are moving through your career slowly? When you get in that mode where everything seems to be dragging to a halt, you need something to snap you out of those doldrums.

You need some momentum motivation! You need something to help drive you forward from point A to B to C and beyond. It needs to be visual and constant.

One thing that has helped me and many other artists who have adopted this method is the following:

Head on over to your favorite office supply store and wander through the calendar aisle. There you'll find those laminated wall calendars with large boxes to write in, perhaps with the months laid out in one long line. You can get one for the upcoming year or better yet, if you can find the ones without any dates, then you can write them in and reuse the calendars year after year. Get two in that case, one for the coming year and then one to use for the next year. Also buy a packet of erasable, colored magic markers.

Now put them up in your workspace so that you have to look at it when you go into that space. You don't want it hidden behind a door or on a back wall you never look at. You want it to hit you in the face constantly.

Fill in the dates in the boxes if you got the blank calendars.

Now comes the fun part. Pick your colors for the following categories:

❖ Confirmed Dates
❖ Dates in the Works
❖ Anchor Events that you are attending, like conferences
❖ Desired Events you want to book, like featured gigs or festivals
❖ Personal Events you plan to attend, like weddings, family gatherings, vacations

Once you've chosen a color for each category begin filling in those dates on your calendars as far into the future as possible. This process may require you to do a bit of research into some of the events you know happen each year, but you are not quite sure of the next year's exact dates. Get those dates and fill them in. As soon as you get information about a personal event, like a family gathering, place that on your calendar.

Now with all known things filled in, you have a visual reminder of what's coming up and a visual motivator to help you see further out into your future for the next two years.

Now you can begin strategically planning your future by beginning to surround those anchor dates with other gigs. Once you get into this habit of adding to the calendar and using the calendar to spark new tour ideas, you will always be creating momentum and booking tours further and further out into the future. You will never be at a loss for where to book new gigs or what to promote next. The calendars will move you forward, helping you prioritize what to do next. December is a great month to begin this process as you prepare for the New Year coming up.

Biz Booster #31
Are You Stuck in a Rut?

As you review how you have managed your business over the last four years, can you identify one thing you have been doing repeatedly to achieve desired outcomes? Is there one way you have been booking your dates or making your calls or marketing your act? Has it been working time and again?

Are you satisfied with the results you've been achieving? If you are, then please identify that method or strategy and repeat it often in everything you do.

BUT, if it has not delivered the results you are after, then again, identify that strategy or method, isolate it and let's really examine it. Your attempt to use a method or strategy that is not working may just be the one thing keeping you stuck in your rut.

You may have heard the expression, "The definition of crazy is doing the same thing over and over again expecting a different outcome." Perhaps it is time to take a second look at some of the ways in which you do some of your activities. Perhaps you are not seeing some of the growth you would like because you are expecting a different outcome using the same activities that didn't meet your needs in the first place.

Let's break down your activities, and please add to this short list if there are activities you do which are not listed here.

❖ Booking
❖ Marketing
❖ Planning

- Working with team members
- Working with group members
- Creating your art
- Collaborating with other artists or industry professionals

Now take each item on the list and break down your methods or strategies that you use to accomplish these items. For example, let's take booking. Perhaps you work with an agent, in this case identify how you communicate and plan with your agent. If you book yourself, look at how you schedule your time to make calls, do follow-up, issue contracts, search for new potential gigs and plan your tours. Each activity requires some method, some plan of action and how you go about accomplishing this activity.

When you break down your activities and methods in this way, you will be able to recognize the activities, strategies or methods that work and those that do not. Once you do that, you are more able to seek out new strategies to replace those not working and make the fundamental changes in your career that you need to move forward and get unstuck from your rut to create a more successful business.

Biz Booster #32
Low Hanging Fruit

A few years ago I was walking my dog past an undeveloped lot with lots of overgrown bushes. As I looked up after cleaning up his business, I was hit on the head with a bunch of thorn branches weighed down with ripe juicy blackberries. I couldn't believe my luck. I walked past this spot many times and just never saw the unripe berries, right there getting ready for picking.

Thanks to my dog and needing to pay attention to his business, my day was made so much sweeter since I was forced to look at my surroundings much more carefully.

I ran home to get some containers and came back to the spot for a blackberry-picking spree. Then, for the next two weeks or so, I made sure to bring along some extra bags to pick some berries every day until they were done. Now, every year at this time, I keep my eyes open as I come to that lot to catch those berries as soon as they are ripe. Each time I pick them, I thank my dog for helping me make the discovery.

Here are some questions for. Are you too focused on picking up YOUR business that you are not paying attention to YOUR surroundings? Do you look up and out to see what's right in front of you that you might have missed the day before?

There may be opportunities staring you in the face or bopping you on the head with a thorn bush. Are you able to see them and take advantage of them?

Remember to pick your head up from your business and look around, look up and down. There may just be some low hanging fruit ready for the picking in your world. Don't miss them. They may only be ripe for the picking for a very short time.

Biz Booster #33
Stay Focused

How many times in a week does someone mention something to you about what they are doing or where they are touring or a project they are involved with? For a split second you think, "Wow, it would be cool to do that." Or, "Maybe I should tour there." Or "I should get involved with that too."

And then, I hope you take a breath and really think about it and consider whether this thing, this tour, this project is *really what you want to do*. Is it something that moves you forward towards *your* goals?

We get so-called "opportunities" coming at us all the time. I like to really look at them from all directions and see whether they are actually opportunities or distractions. So many distractions are all dressed up looking just like an opportunity. You have got to recognize the difference.

Here's a tip to help you see whether that sheep knocking at your door is really a wolf about to blow your house down.

Step one: Get all the information you can about this so called, "opportunity." (Or all the information you care to spend time on right now.)

Step two: Review your goals for your immediate future. Is this opportunity in line with your immediate goals for the next three months?

Step three: Review your long-term goals. Does this opportunity fit well with your long-term goals? Will taking time to focus on this opportunity now, drive you closer to your long-term goals down the road, or will it take you down a completely different path which may not be in alignment with who you are and what you are all about?

After looking closely at these three steps, your heart will be singing to you and telling you exactly what to do. I get an ache in the pit of my stomach that tells me I'm looking at something that just doesn't feel right for me. I've learned to pay attention to those aches.

You may have a different signal that lets you know something is not quite right. Learn your signals. Obey them. They just might save you from making some very bad decisions.

Pay attention to all those "opportunities" coming at you and make sure they are not out to test you and distract you from YOUR goals and YOUR focus and YOUR purpose.

Biz Booster #34
Creativity vs Productivity

Which comes first, creativity or productivity? As a musician and performing artist, I would venture a guess that the creator in you was the driving force that led you to become a performing artist.

OK, let's back up a bit. First let me break open the Webster's Dictionary and define these two terms so we can be on the same page.

Creativity: *noun,* The use of the imagination or original ideas, esp. in the production of an artistic work.

Productivity: *noun,* A measure relating a quantity or quality of output to the inputs required to produce it.

Now with these definitions in mind, I'd like to make a few observations and then a few suggestions.

Observation #1: You do the work you do because you are a creator and are creative.

Observation #2: There are a lot of distractions within the performing arts business that keep you from your creativity.

Observation #3: When you focus on productivity rather than creativity, the art and the business suffer because your whole reason for doing the business, sharing your creativity, loses its momentum and drive. Productivity factors such as how many CDs you have sold, how many gigs are booked, how many Facebook fans you have, or even how many tweets you've sent can leave you feeling out of sorts and divorced from your artistic self.

Suggestion #1: Refocus on creativity. Let your creative side become a momentum-driver for your business. How do you do this? You start with creativity each day. Your art must come first. Creating your art must take priority in the service of selling your art.

Suggestion #2: Allow the creative in you to drive your priorities and help set your goals. Go for quality rather than quantity. Quality art demands quality venues, appreciative fans and respectable fees.

Suggestion #3: Set your creative bar high. The more attention you put to becoming the best creator of your art you can be, the more your art will be valued and in demand. There is a lot of competition out there and the cream will rise to the top, will sell more CDs and get better gigs for higher fees.

Conclusion: When you focus on creativity, as an artist, this reaffirms who you are and why you get up each day. When you put your art first, your enthusiasm to sell your art will flow more easily, even more creatively. If you are excited about your latest song or tune or piece of writing, you will be more motivated to get it in front of the right audience. When you wake up each day, hungry to create or learn to be a better creator, then your motivation to get better gigs to share your latest creation will drive your business forward.

I'd say creativity comes well before productivity. Let it be your driving factor first. *Your art deserves it.*

Business

Biz Booster #35
Getting Help in Your Office—
Where to Find Help

I hope you have your list of tasks to delegate from Biz Booster #16 and have written your job description. Now let's explore some possible resources and places to find your potential assistant.

For those of you living in or near a university town, there are a number of options involving internships. The departments that I would check into are:

❖ MBA Programs in Business & Marketing
❖ Arts Management Programs
❖ Business Departments
❖ Journalism Departments
❖ Theater Departments
❖ Music Business, but not the music departments

The **Music & Entertainment Industry Educators Association,** MEIEA, (http://www.meiea.org), includes over eighty-five schools across the country having music business programs. Here you may find eager students who are interested in the business-side of the industry and would welcome a real-life experience working for a performing artist.

With any of the above departments I would contact the department's chair and discuss your interests in grooming a student intern. I would look for a student who is near the beginning of their studies, so you have an opportunity work with them for a couple of years rather than train someone about to graduate. By becoming involved with a school that has a music business curriculum, you may be able to propose projects you are planning as a case study, thereby getting some free help and advice and a chance to try some of your new ideas.

Beyond universities, local, regional and state arts councils have ListServes where you may list your job description. People searching for work in the arts, review those postings and you may connect with someone who is already familiar with the music and performing arts industry.

You may also find someone already interested in you from your mailing list. I would include your job description in an email to your list. This call for support may bring some friendly inquiries as well as referrals from your fan base to their friends who may be looking for some part-time work.

Biz Booster #36
Getting Help in Your Office—The Interview

Here are three things you must do when interviewing a prospective assistant. Pull out your list of tasks and job description before you conduct any interview to create your list of talking points or questions.

First: Plan on having three phone interviews before having an in-person interview. If you are working with a virtual assistant (someone who is not in your area and who will not be working from your office), then skip the in-person interview and add a fourth phone interview. Having three short phone interviews helps build a relationship before you commit to a relationship. Why do phone interviews? Your assistant may immediately or eventually be making lots of calls on your behalf. You can tell right away whether this person has a great phone personality and can think on their feet. If your phone interview with them is lack-luster, why invest your time and money to have them represent you.

You want someone who already has developed a winning personality so you can capitalize on that talent while training them to do your work.

Second: Plan on short interviews of no more than thirty to forty-five minutes each. Divide your questions into three categories to be asked during each of the three interviews.

Category 1: The "Get to Know Them and Cut to the Chase" Interview. Why are they interested in working for you? Have they had any experience doing the kind of work you need? Mostly though, you want to experience their phone manner. You should be able to determine on this first call whether it's even worth having another call. If you don't get the kind of information you are looking for in the experience department or if you feel uncomfortable with their phone manner, thank them and move on to another person.

Category 2: The "Confident Enough to Schedule the Second" Interview. If you're confident that a second interview is appropriate, schedule one for either later that day or the next day or in as short a time frame as possible. Give yourself time to think about your first conversation and make notes about subjects you would like to revisit or cover in more depth.

This next call should cover questions about their long range goals for work and family, the length of time they could commit to working with you, as well as their available hours. This call allows them to demonstrate more personality and enthusiasm as they talk about their own life. You'll continue to get an idea of how they interact on the phone. Do they have enthusiasm for their life's plans and can you see how that might transfer to how they'll represent you? Do their future plans mean they'll leave you shortly or is there potential for this to grow into a long-term working relationship worthy of you investing your time and money? Do they show interest in finding out more about your work and the job they'll be doing for you— do they ask interesting questions?

Category 3: The "Third Call is the Charm" Interview. If you've reached three calls, there is a good chance that this person might be right for your job. This call is your opportunity to share some of your goals for working with an assistant and get a feel for their interest to grow with you. If all sounds good on this call, it's time to meet in person if you will be working in person and if not then it's time to make some decisions.

Third: The third and most important part of the interview process, is for you to demonstrate a calm enthusiasm for your business. Do not overwhelm the interviewee with your desire to dump all of your unwanted tasks on them during the interview. Be cautious not to scare them away by giving them the impression that your livelihood depends on them. Remember, you want to ease someone into your fold, groom them for greater involvement. That's why you made a job description of non-income-producing tasks.

By keeping these three suggestions in mind when interviewing, you will save yourself lots of time and money and hopefully find the perfect assistant. Happy interviewing!

Biz Booster #37
Getting Help in Your Office—What to Pay?

Hire your assistant part-time, six to eight hours a week to get started. This allows them to start working on short projects and for you to get to know each other.

You can increase the hours as needed, but keep it under twenty hours per week.

Hire your assistant as a contract worker that can be counted as an expense on your tax return rather than an employee. This will save you a bundle. Check with your accountant on the tax benefits of expensing a contract worker.

Now, do the math. What can you afford? I generally have paid between $8 and $15 an hour for the type of non-income-producing work I discussed in Biz Booster #16. If I have a project that requires someone with special expertise in a certain field, then I may have to pay more—but on a short-term basis. For the kind of assistance we have been talking about, research, prepping and mailing marketing materials, sending contracts and contacting the media, etc., the dollar amounts above should work well.

Eventually, if your assistant proves to be someone who can do more and accept greater responsibility, and your confidence in their abilities grows with time, then you may consider revamping their job description.

You may begin to have them take on some gig booking responsibilities. If and when this occurs, in one instance I would continue to pay the hourly wage either, add a percentage of the gig's income they booked to the hourly wage, in this case perhaps 5%. Or, pay a percentage of the gig booked OR their hourly wage, whichever is greater and in this case I would use 10%.

Now if you are hiring an intern from a university who is also getting course credit for their work with you, you may be able to reduce your hourly rate. If the intern has potential to stick around for a while, paying a better rate may be just the right incentive necessary to keep them longer.

Biz Booster #38
Organize Your Way into the New Year

Here's a great organizing tip to prepare for the New Year. Each year during the week between Christmas and New Years, when I'm at home, I organize my most used files. This process coincides with my tax prep each year, so in one exercise I accomplish two tasks, getting my files ready for the New Year and getting my taxes ready for my accountant. Cool!

Here's what I do:

❖ I keep some of those collapsible storage boxes with covers up in my attic or get a new batch from a local office supply store.

❖ I make sure I've got some new manila file folders on hand.

❖ I separate my personal from my business files to keep my accountant happy, so I use two boxes.

❖ Starting with my personal files, I go through my file cabinet and put the old file in the box and put a new, similarly labeled file folder in its place in the cabinet. Any information that needs to be kept handy from year to year gets transferred into the new folder. This process continues throughout the personal file drawers and then I move on to do the same with the business drawers.

When completed, I have my file drawers ready for next year's file activity and my two boxes ready for me to go through when I prepare my tax info. It's a quick way to get organized for the New Year while doing my preliminary tax prep. Since it's holiday time, I listen to some cool new holiday music I just picked up to keep a festive party-like mood so it doesn't seem so much like work. When I'm done, I feel ready to take on the New Year.

I hope this little organizing tip gets you ready for your next year. Happy New Year!

Biz Booster #39
Managing Your Career

Are you managing your own career? The devil's in the details? Or perhaps it is really a matter of semantics. Let me explain.

The term "Artist Manager," as it is used in the entertainment industry, will most often mean the person who oversees the "Big Picture" for the artist's development and forward movement toward career success. This means they deal with all the people involved with the artist from agents, publicist, record companies, publishers, travel personnel, group members and in turn deal with all the millions of details related to every one of those team members.

Now according to the dictionary the word manager has five potential meanings:

1. to succeed in accomplishing
2. to take or be in charge of or control of
3. to dominate or influence
4. to be in charge or control of an undertaking
5. to get along, function

So when you think about managing your own career or perhaps another artist's career you are more than likely using one or all of the above definitions as you do your job.

Even though success as a touring artist requires that you do manage all the activities that move you toward your goals, I would like to raise the bar a bit and offer a new way for you to think about your job. What if from now on you view yourself as a *Visionary Entrepreneur?*

The reality is that in order to be a successful artist or artist manager or agent, you need to have a vision of what you would like your future to look like. The other fact is that you *are* an entrepreneur running your own business. When you combine the two words, you plant the seeds for something far greater and much more impressive than simply managing your activities.

A Visionary Entrepreneur uses their imagination to create opportunities that open new doors. A Visionary Entrepreneur sees possibilities for new collaborations. A Visionary Entrepreneur has an overview of their business, keenly aware of their past history, strategically involved with their present circumstance and able to use both adeptly to design their future. They know what they would like to accomplish and are savvy enough to surround themselves with the right people to help them.

This week, raise your head high above all the minutia of your day-to-day, and look around you. How can you transform yourself from the manager of your career into a Visionary Entrepreneur? What twist of thought might it take to raise the bar for your own career? What act of creativity, self confidence or action might be required to stop simply managing your activities and become your own Visionary Entrepreneur? Might not this be one way of taking your touring career to the next level?

CD Sales

Biz Booster #40
How to Sell More CDs at Your Live Shows

Think about the concept of inviting the audience to meet you at the merchandise table. Invite them to come by and say hello. You would love to hear their thoughts about the show and personalize a CD for them.

Now most artists mention that they have CDs at a table somewhere in the venue. They don't always say they'll be at the table. Most artists mention that this song or that song is on the CD that is on that table somewhere in the venue. And some artists mention that this song or that song is on the CD on the table somewhere in the venue in between every single song throughout the night. Let's face it, it can get old and very uninteresting.

The most successful artists at selling their products are the one's who really plan their pitch, make it interesting and time it appropriately within the set at various intervals. Think about your pitch and weave it strategically throughout your set. However, the absolutely most successful people at selling are the one's who invite their audience to meet them and say hello. The one's who take the time at intermission and make themselves accessible and tell their audience that they are doing just that before the end of each set, are the one's who sell really well at each gig.

If you are an independent artist who relies on CD sales as an important part of your income, you have got to create a great pitch, invite your audience to meet you and buy your merchandise and you cannot be shy about it. You must be clever, accessible and genuine. When you are, your sales will grow.

Biz Booster #41
Planning a CD Release & Tour—Step One

Determine the scope of your capabilities based on where you are right now in your career and what you would like to achieve within this next year. Let the following factors guide your plans.

Budget: Did you include money in your budget for marketing and touring? How much did you set aside for sending CDs to print, broadcast and Internet media? The larger this budget, the more extensive your campaign can be in a shorter period of time, perhaps you may even use outside promotions companies.

If you don't have a huge budget set, don't worry, you just need to be more strategic and refined in your scope of outreach over an extended period of time. This approach can help you reach your target audience more effectively in the long run.

Expand your market: To open new markets may require some investments. So rather than spending money you haven't budgeted to conquer the whole country try the following.

Focus on one or two areas where you currently have a strong following. Build tours using those places as a central starting point and work your way out from that center. Study my articles on "Developing a Home Base of Support" (https://performingbiz.com/developing-home-base-support-build-national-success-part-2), and use that template to begin building in new markets.

Concentrate your media marketing in those areas supporting specific dates to develop a strong statewide, then regional following.

Let your first steps to any release planning focus on the successes you already have and grow from there. You will use your finances more efficiently as you build a solid foundation in a central region that you can return to often.

Biz Booster #42
Planning a CD Release & Tour—Step Two

Now that you've determined the scope of your campaign, the next thing to do is make sure you have a great story to tell. Your story is what will get the press to write about you and your CD.

It's not enough these days to let the CD release be the story. The competition for review space and airplay is just overwhelming. So, write a list of at least five interesting things about you, your group, or your CD that tell a unique story and then create a press release about each point of interest.

Perhaps there is a theme running throughout the songs you write or record; maybe you and your band mates started playing together in elementary school; perhaps there is a song on the CD that was written for a specific purpose or cause; maybe you overcame great challenges in your life and now turned to writing about them; perhaps you perform to a unique niche audience and that is of interest; maybe someone associated with the CD is a well-known person and your association with them might make a unique story. Dig deep, look for something that the press will find interesting to their readers and want to interview you, as well as review the CD. Give the radio DJs something unique to talk about while cueing up a track.

Once they get to the music, hopefully it will speak for itself and entice the writer or DJ to promote it, but you have to compel them to open the CD and listen and your press release with a great story is your key to reviews and airplay.

Even if you decide to work with a publicist or a radio promotions company, you need to give them a great story to help promote you and have success with the campaign.

If you are not releasing a new CD, but still selling a current CD, this exercise will help you open the new markets where you want to play. This exercise will change the scope of your campaign and all of your marketing if you do this each time you have a new project or tour or release.

Biz Booster #43
Planning a CD Release & Tour-Step Three

Now that you have a great story or even a few great stories, the next step is to make your CD Release and Tour more of a media event. These next two ideas will help you do just that.

Give this Release and Tour a Theme. Look at the songs, is there a theme running through your writing? Do you have a particular focus or point you want to make with this CD and tour? Name your tour with a catchy phrase that the media will latch on to. Do something interesting, unique, attention grabbing that is bound to get the media involved. Check my article to learn "How To Turn Gigs Into Major Media Events," (http://performingbiz.com/turn-gigs-into-media-events) for more in-depth ideas.

Attach Your CD Release and Tour to a Cause. This takes planning, but is absolutely the way to get major media and general audience attention. It's best to find an organization whose cause you are passionate about and one that has chapters in many cities in your region, nationally or even internationally. When you work with an organization for a cause, you benefit from the extra attention while the media focuses on the cause. By planning well in advance for each concert, you enjoy the added assistance from the organization's internal marketing network as well as their connections to the communities in which they are based.

Another plus to this method, is that many venues may become more open to hiring you when they know that the event has a greater potential for ticket sales, media and community outreach. My article, "Benefit from Playing Benefits," (https://performingbiz.com/benefiting-playing-benefits) goes into more depth on this topic.

With so many CDs being released independently, you have got to plan something more interesting to capture the attention of the media and your audience. I hope you will add one or both of these methods to your strategic planning.

Biz Booster #44
Selling CDs in Bulk

Are you selling your CDs one at a time? Do you have some old CDs that you haven't sold yet and they are just sitting there taking up space?

Here is another way to move some of those CDs, whether old or new. It's not just about moving them or selling them, it's more about getting your music into the hands of an unlikely audience—a new audience. OK how?

You may play benefits for charitable organizations, private events like weddings, corporate events for a local business or parties of any sort. C'mon admit it, every once in a while you do one of these kinds of gigs. Perhaps you do these kinds of gigs all the time. And I bet you think that these gigs are *no CD sales* gigs. Well think again!

This is a prime opportunity to sell more CDs than you might imagine. Let's break this down into action steps.

Step 1: While you are working on your booking and negotiating the gig details, ask if they would like to make their event even more memorable by giving a gift to commemorate the occasion.

Step 2: Get some info about the people or the organization and the event being planned.

Now if it's a charitable organization, you might suggest that one of their sponsors purchase your CD for a discount and a tax write off. (I'll leave the discount amount up to you, but 40 or 50% off might be nice). Then they can resell the CD to all their supporters for full price as a fundraiser. They look good and you look good and you get your CD to some new listeners and potential new fans.

For other types of gigs, like weddings or business gigs, they can purchase bulk CDs to hand out as favors for weddings or gifts for business. Just think, for a wedding, that could be 100 CDs or more at 50% off or even more if you're feeling the love, you still are going to have a much better pay-day in the long run.

When folks are in the planning mode for a wedding or party, they are likely going to spend money on some trinket anyway, so why not something that might have a bit more meaning and one that the recipient will reuse often. You can mention that when they play your CD, they'll remember the event fondly, especially if a song on the CD is one you sang live at the reception or ceremony.

For the business event, just mention how the company's good-will, will be appreciated by all who attended the event, each time the worker plays the CD.

Step 3: Remember to do this each time you are invited to perform at an event where you think CD sales will be unlikely. Turn each of these no-CD sales gigs into a CD sales bonanza.

College Bookings

Biz Booster #45
Multiple Performance Opportunities
on Campus

If you live in a college town, then you may be used to the rise and fall of the population as students come and go during the year. Streets get crowded, restaurants are packed and hotels are booked during those college event-filled weekends. You know the ones, home-coming weekend, graduation, of course, and then there are the home games during the favorite sport of the season.

So how does all this affect your performing career? If you want to make a connection with the college market, you might spend some time getting to know the flow of their schedule, when they might be likely to book special events to coincide with events that occur on a regular basis each year.

By visiting the school's website you'll easily find the academic calendar, listing events, home games and any major department events that have already been put on the schedule. If you dig a bit deeper, into individual departments, such as the Theater Department or Student Activities, you'll soon discover specially scheduled events that you may be able to tap into or time frames that you ought to avoid as you make your plans.

The potential for gigs on a college campus doesn't just rest with the Student Activities Office and the coffeehouse or concert committee. Special activities are scheduled throughout the year for functions within each department, fraternity or sorority parties, meetings within the administration office or within various staff offices for different schools such as Law, Medical Center, Engineering, Music or Education, etc.

The university campus offers a creatively-thinking artist a myriad of opportunities beyond the obvious ones. With a little research and some understanding of the school's calendar, a number of performances, workshop or master-class opportunities may be available on a single college campus.

If you are lucky enough to live in or near a college town, it will be worth your while to begin exploring all that may be possible right in your own backyard.

Biz Booster #46
Working with Student Activities

The most visible event producer on a college campus is the Student or Campus Activities Office. There is always a Campus Activities Director who ultimately signs the contracts and essentially designs the events calendar. This person is also the student advisor for the various student committees that help plan the events.

Some of the student committees that you may have come in contact with are the Concert Committee that produces large concert events, a coffeehouse committee that produces smaller events, a lecture committee that helps produce a variety of lecture programs with famous speakers, authors, newsy or noteworthy people, to name just a few. These three committees are the ones you will most likely work with as you attempt to line up a performance through the Student Activities Office.

Here are some insights to help you navigate the often frustrating experience of dealing with student committees.

Always find out who the Student Activities Director is and who the Faculty Advisor is for your specific committee. By knowing the faculty person who is ultimately responsible for signing the contract, you maintain contact with a person you can connect with when contacting the student committee member becomes difficult.

Students on committees often rotate every semester. This is a fact that can frustrate your efforts to finalize a booking. With committee members changing, irregular office hours and students who are basically doing this for fun; a professional performing artist must put up with making a lot of extra phone calls to track down your student booker before finalizing a date.

Since you are the professional in this instance, you may find yourself spending some time educating the students about how to best book and present your act. This is just part of the process when working with college campuses.

As the student body changes from one semester to the next, so do the entertainment tastes, fads and fashion. What might have been hot on campus one semester is passé the next.

Here are a few benefits you can look forward to when working through a Campus Activities office:

They have student money that needs to be spent each semester or they don't get as much the following semester. They don't need to make money in some instances. There are some campuses that run a professional club and have professional bookers, paid student wait staff and tech crews. They run these clubs like a business. It is at these campus clubs where I have always preferred to book my acts.

Working through the activities office helps you break into a new market with a paid gig, gives you access to campus radio and newspaper and does not preclude your contacting the local media for additional off-campus marketing.

Campus Activities has been a place where many major artists get their start. It is these very college student committee members whose interests in the latest styles, fads and new talent, that helps bring attention to little know emerging acts and gives them a venue.

I know I'll date myself now, but it was at my college campus coffee house where an unknown John Denver played one of his first gigs. And it was at my community college where a then very young Bruce Springsteen and the E Street Band played one of their first concerts. I also recall being at a showcase for Campus Activities in NYC where I saw a fresh out of college comic, Billy Crystal, do a stand up routine that eventually landed him on Saturday Night Live. As they say, the rest is history.

Lastly, campus gigs help you tour while making money. They allow you to intersperse well-paying college gigs with career-building promotional, opening or showcase gigs.

So as frustrating and as rewarding as working with Student Activities student committees may be, it may also be a worthwhile career investment.

Biz Booster #47
Working with Campus
Performing Arts Centers

Next to the student activities office, the campus performing arts center may be the next largest producer of events. These events, however, are mostly booked by the performing arts program or artistic director rather than a student committee. The director may also be connected to the theater department.

Performances booked into this facility tend to include theatre, classical concerts, and other genres of music that the student activities office generally doesn't book. Productions booked into the performing arts center may also include shows for children where schools bus their students in and season series that cater to a campus and community audience.

Shows booked into the performing arts center are generally booked twelve to eighteen months in advance. The program director may be an active member of a presenting organization or network that hosts booking conferences and showcases. They may do a majority of their booking by attending a regional conference such as Western Arts Alliance (http://www.westarts.org) or a national conference such as APAP—Association of Performing Arts Presenters (http://www.artspresenters.org). These conferences are well attended by performing arts center programmers nationally and internationally and many of the programmers rely on the attending agents to provide them with the bulk of their talent.

If your act is appropriate for a performing arts center venue, then there are two options for you to explore in order to get a booking.

1. When you are ready, check out one of the regional presenter booking conferences closest to you.
2. Explore your region for college campuses that have a performing art centers and book them on your own. You can often find a listing of these venues through your state arts council. They have a database or a presenter's network on the state agency website. Not only will this give you a great listing of potential venues, but you may also learn what benefits the state arts council offers performers in your state. Many state and provincial arts councils, have artists' tour directories which the presenting organizations reference to

find talent for their programs. Applying to be on these council tour directories is a step in establishing your credibility with many of these performing arts centers.

A review of a performing arts centers' website will give you the contact person and a wealth of information about the venue and their past and current season's programming. This can help you determine if this, in fact, is an appropriate venue to pursue a booking.

You can call directly, without an agent and without having been to a conference and you should call, and get your act on their radar. These programmers are always looking for new acts to offer to their audiences. But, they are also more concerned with selling their tickets, filling their halls and making money. Many of these centers do apply for and receive grants from the state arts councils, the university and private donations, but they still need to make their budget. The programmers are savvy negotiators who have been booking talent for a long time. They are professionals as compared to the student committee members on the concert or coffeehouse committees. So in the case of dealing with performing arts centers, you need to have your *A-game* on with your materials and your pitch, professionally presented.

Conferences

Biz Booster #48
Choosing Appropriate Conferences to Attend

With so many conferences vying for your dollar, promising you access to bookings, media and record deals, you need to make choices based on two things at first.

1. Where are you currently building your audience?

Are you still trying to grow in your region or have you begun to expand nationally or internationally? Now just because you may want to be a national or international act, doesn't mean you're there yet, or that you are ready to jump ahead and take on the whole country. Grow at a pace that you can keep up with and attend conferences that are appropriate for where you are in your stage of development as an artist. By doing this you make contact with venue bookers, media and industry professionals in the areas where you want to develop a following.

When you attend a conference that caters to a larger area or larger venues than you are ready for, it's overwhelming, frustrating and, in most cases, can be a waste of your money attempting such a large leap. You just may not yet have the resources available to take advantage of all the opportunities.

2. Who attends the conferences you are considering?

Check with the conference organizer and ask for a

break down of last year's attendees. You want to know the number of artists, venue bookers, festival bookers, record labels or print and broadcast media who attended. If you're going to conferences to find new venues, colleges or festivals to play, you want to make sure the percentage of bookers from those venues attending is at least equal to or greater than the percentage of artists like yourself. Attending a booking conference where most of the attendees are artists looking for gigs, will turn out to be an expensive party with little opportunity to showcase your act to those who can make a difference in your career, like book you for a gig.

Choose conferences that have the potential to meet your goals. For more in-depth information about attending conferences, showcasing and exhibiting at trade shows, check out my articles, "Attending Booking Conferences Parts 1" (https://performingbiz.com/attending-booking-conferences-part-1-showcasing) and "Part 2." (https://performingbiz.com/attending-booking-conferences-part-2-trade-show)

Biz Booster #49
Booking Conference Guidance

So much attention gets directed toward sending out advanced emails or printing postcards and posters listing your upcoming showcases. But, have you put much attention to planning your time to maximize your effectiveness at the conference? It's great to party and play in all your friend's hotel rooms or showcase rooms, but is that where the bookers or media are hanging out?

Here are three strategies you can use to get the most out of your conference experience.

First, set some goals before you leave for the conference. What do you hope to accomplish by attending this conference?

Is it a booking conference? Do you want to get gigs? If that's one goal, then make sure you attend workshops where the bookers will be speaking on panels. Don't be shy, ask questions and go up there and meet them after the workshop. Put a face to the name and put your face in front of them.

Is it a media conference? Do you want to get your CD to radio, introduce yourself to writers and show hosts? Make sure you attend any workshops where those people might gather.

Second, access the attendee directory. As soon as you get the conference attendee directory, go through it and highlight the people, organizations and events that you want to meet or attend. Create a time line in your own calendar to remind you of those events and make sure you attend them. Showcases, exhibit hall time and social events are all great places to meet those folks on your target list. But, workshops are really the only place you might be able to match a panel participant with one of the people you specifically desire to meet. If you have access to the directory of attendees prior to the conference you can also set up specific meetings with your target list of people.

Third, plan your meetings. Have a plan for when you meet those on your list as to how you will introduce yourself and what you might give them. Make it memorable. If you don't create a plan ahead of time, you will be at a loss for words or how to direct the conversation and you may very well lose a great opportunity. These greetings don't have to be forced or insincere, rather simply be prepared with a conversation opener, an introduction and perhaps a plan to maintain a connection with the person after the conference is over.

By approaching the conference with these three steps in mind, you will turn an overwhelming event into a pocketful of future opportunities.

Biz Booster #50
Negative Aspects of Conferences

Let's examine some of the negative aspects of attending conferences. Face it, conferences are expensive and sometimes they end up being an expensive party rather than a good career boost.

As you decide which conferences to attend, check these following items, with the conference organizers before signing up, since this info may not be on the website for public display:

1. How many years has the conference been happening?
2. What were the turn outs last year and the year before?
3. Get the breakdown of artists, bookers, media and industry such as record labels, publishers, publicists, agents, managers, etc.
4. How many showcasing artists are they accepting? Does this number present too much competition?
5. Are the showcases juried and produced by the conference or self-produced in hotel rooms or other venues? Will producing your own showcase add to your expenses while diminishing your chances of being seen by the appropriate people?
6. How many exhibitors were there last year? Of those how many were agents or self- managed artists? Again what does this do to raise the competition factor?
7. What are the registration fees or showcase fees?
8. Do you get a sound check if you showcase?
9. Will attending the conference take away good paying gig dates that you can ill afford at this time?

Examine your goals, your budget, your costs, and then scrutinize the percentages of the categories of people who generally attend. If you truly think the opportunities are realistic based on the kind of attendees regularly coming to the event, then you have a much better chance of making the conference work for you. But, if there are more artists than bookers or media, you may just be wasting you time and money, even though it might be a great time.

Conventions: Potential Gigs & New Audiences

Organizations, businesses and groups, large and small, tend to gather in a meeting place once, twice or several times throughout the year. Some will travel to cities with large convention centers and others tend to find a smaller hotel or meeting space. Two things are always true of these gatherings. There is always someone associated with the organization who is the coordinator of the meeting, conference or convention and there is always a conference liaison working with that organization from the hotel, conference or convention center.

Often, the organization holding the conference is open to or actively seeking an entertainment element to add to the conference and lighten the intensity of the hard word done throughout the day.

If you live near a town with an obvious convention center taking up blocks of city space, such as in Nashville or New Orleans, then you may find it easier to contact the convention liaison. But, if you live in or near a town without an obvious convention center, then you may need to check with local hotels, meeting halls or catering halls to make contact with a local conference or convention liaison.

One of the benefits of working with a conference liaison at a convention or conference center or hotel is that they know who has booked their space often years in advance. By getting to know the conference liaisons at various centers and getting on their list of entertainers to call and refer, you may have the potential to book many gigs far in advance. These may serve as your anchor dates for tours farther from home or steady work close to home. Because these conferences need to be planned so far in advance, this also gives you plenty of time to contact the organization and establish a connection with their conference coordinator or entertainment and programming committee.

I know a musician in New Orleans who is the go-to artist that the New Orleans Convention Center calls all the time. He works constantly for great money playing to new audiences and sleeps at home every night.

If you live near a convention or conference center, this may be one way to build new audiences, tap into a potential niche market that could serve you beyond the actual conference gig and give you steady work closer to your home base. And to top it all off, these conferences and conventions often have sizable entertainment programming budgets. So price yourself appropriately. Ask their budget first, plan you pricing, then state your fee.

I encourage you to look around your region for obvious and not so obvious conference and convention centers. Make a list of up to five potential places and check them out. Make an appointment with their conference liaison to bring them your packet or even offer to do a showcase for them. This could set you up with ongoing gigs for many years to come, gaining new audiences in potentially new niche markets.

Contracts

Biz Booster #52
Contracts—Why You Need Them

I read a lot of emails that talk about getting burned by venues because there was no contract on the date. You worked so hard to get the gig. Now you need to make sure it is real!

Trust is a wonderful thing and you want to trust the booker who gave you the date. You want to trust they will promote the date, that you'll be on their website's calendar list of upcoming events, that they will pay you at the end of the gig the amount and the percentage that you discussed and agreed to on the phone or in your email.

The way to make sure that all of those things happen is to issue a contract. Don't get scared because the word *contract* sounds like you have to fill your contract with legalese. You need to simply document the details. A contract is simply a written history of your agreement. It doesn't have to be long and filled with complicated language, (although there is a reason for that language).

For now, you just have to create something that helps you and the person booking you, document what you discussed and agreed to and you need to do this each and every time you book a date. Once you have something in writing that states all of the details you discussed, you each sign and have a copy of this agreement, then you are speaking the same language and your trust is now bound by something you can each refer to later.

If you have a question about something that you thought would be taken care of, but wasn't, you can look at the contract and say, "That was your job," or "That was my job."

Mostly, it will give you peace of mind that you are supposed to be somewhere on a specific date at a specific time to play. And you will know, for sure, that they will be waiting for you, expecting you, will hopefully have promoted your gig and will, at the end of the performance, pay you what you agreed.

As far as how to write your contract and what kind of document you need, I'll refer you one of my articles, "The Right Documents for Booking Gigs" (https://performingbiz.com/right-documents-booking-gigs) and my package of Contract Forms (https://performingbiz.com/product/booking-contract-forms).

Whatever contract you use, please begin using something to document your agreements for every gig you book. This one act can raise your level of professionalism and help you begin to be taken seriously.

Biz Booster #53
Deposits—A Down Payment on Your Gig

If you are making $500 or more at a gig, then you should be asking for a deposit. When you ask for a deposit, you are asking the venue to make a commitment to your gig. If they have money invested up front, it is more likely that they will do more to make the gig a success.

A deposit is a percentage of the total guarantee. Normally, the industry standard is 50% of the guarantee, but it doesn't have to be. You may decide on any percentage that works for you and the booking person. In some instances, an agent making a 15% or 20%

commission may ask for at least that amount as the deposit if the venue is unable to do the traditional 50%. For the agent, that means, at least they have covered their commission on the date.

If you are booking yourself, begin to ask for some deposit amount at venues that are able to accommodate you.

Performing arts centers, concert promoters, private events and small concert series are likely venues used to providing deposits. On the other hand, universities and colleges, school districts, government organizations, some night clubs and bars are venues less likely or unlikely to pay a deposit. If you are playing for a percentage of the door with no guarantee whatsoever, then a deposit is out of the question.

So review the types of venues you currently play and consider whether getting a deposit makes sense for your current venue type and the size of the guarantees you are getting. If it's a fit, then decide on the percentage of the guarantee that you will ask for as a deposit.

If you never get a guarantee lower than $500.00, then select a standard deposit percentage such as 25%, 35% or 50% of the guarantee. Start including a talking point about your deposit requirement during your negotiation discussions and then make sure to add a deposit clause to your standard contract.

Biz Booster #54
Deposits—Five Important Facts about Taking Deposits

Now that you are thinking about taking deposits, let me offer five important facts you need to know about deposits, how they work and some legal requirements to keep you financially secure.

1. **Your contract clause:** Add a clause to your contract that states the exact amount of the deposit and who it should be made out to. Specify that the deposit is due with the returned contract and the date they are both due back. Make this date no more than fourteen days from the date you sent the contract. That's plenty of time for them to receive it, review it, sign it, make out a check and return it. If the deposit is due on a different date, separate from the contract return date, then specify that date in this clause. Sometimes it's necessary to have a different deposit due date.

2. **What to do with the deposit check?** Deposits are supposed to be put into an escrow account. This account is supposed to be separate from your regular business checking or savings account. It is important to separate this money, so you won't spend it either intentionally or accidentally.

3. **Deposits remain untouched until the date is played.** Your deposit money is a guarantee on your contracted date. It guarantees that you'll show up and play the date and the venue will promote the date and pay you the balances due. The deposit is not travel money to pay for airline tickets to get to the gig. It is not money to pay for anything until the date is played.

4. **Once the date is played** and you collect the balance due and perhaps any percentages above the balance, then you may do whatever is necessary with the deposit money. So, if your agent collected the deposit check and held it, they may now take their commission from that money and send you the rest. If you collected the deposit and need to pay your agent their commission, now you may do so. After the date is successfully finished, you may take the deposit from the separate account it was held in and do with it what you want.

5. **What if the date was cancelled or did not happen?** This is exactly why you need to hold the deposit and

not touch it until the date is played. You may need to return the deposit if the cancellation is legit and in accordance with any cancellation clause you have in your contract. If the date is rescheduled, then you may continue to hold the deposit until the new date is played. If the venue cancels and there is a problem with the time frame in which they cancel, you may be able to keep the deposit even though you won't play the date, *(if you have a cancellation clause in your contract that is specific!)*

I know some of this can get a bit involved in legal aspects, but after all it is your livelihood. If it's necessary to protect your bookings in order to build a successful career, then let's get professional and if necessary, gaining a touch of legal business savvy, couldn't hurt!

Negotiation

Biz Booster #55
Track Your Shows

Do you search for just the right things to say when you are speaking to a venue booker? Try using your numbers to make your case. Start keeping track of your numbers at each gig.

1. Take an accurate count of paid people at each show along with the ticket price and the venue's capacity.
2. Keep a record of all merchandise sales; CDs, t-shirts and whatever else you sell.
3. Make a note of the temperature and weather conditions on that day.
4. Keep records of any other events taking place in town that day that might influence the turnout at your show.

You may already be tracking this information, but are you using it to make a difference where it counts? Now, when you speak to the booker at that venue for a return gig or to a booker at another venue, you have some meaningful information in the form of numbers to leverage your way to a booking. Numbers speak volumes to a booker. Track your shows so you can use your numbers to get future bookings.

Biz Booster #56
Negotiation Technique: How to Reduce the "Call Me Next Week" Syndrome

Let's face it, people are busy with their own agendas and are not always ready to work on your agenda, even when you think you set an appointment. It can be very frustrating to get the booking person to deal with you when you want them to and be ready to work with you to book your gig. So you have to set your own deadlines. Allow yourself three call opportunities to get them on board to work with you.

First Call: Perhaps it's the introduction, you send your promotional material, set another call-back time and along with that, alert them to your deadline. For example: "I need to have all my dates lined up by the end of next week as my marketing pieces go out then." Insert a sense of urgency, a need to move along with your negotiations. If you leave your time-line for confirmation open-ended, then the booking person has no particular need or urgency to confirm. Most likely, they are waiting for another act to confirm with them, so as far as they are concerned, that other act is the important one on their agenda.

Also, give them a specific date or date-range that is of interest to you. Don't just call for any open date. Even if your schedule is wide-open, make sure you offer some specific dates. This sends the message that you are busy.

You need to be ready to have three possible things happen and be OK with any one of them.

1. They may tell you to call back next week. Here's where you remind them of your marketing deadline and attempt to get at least a hold on a date. Then set another call-back for no more than two days away, not next week, to reinforce your urgency.

2. They may give you the date you are looking for or a date in the time-frame you are looking for. Great, book it.
3. Or they may say they are not interested in that date or time-frame since you've indicated a deadline. In this case, be ready with an alternative date or time-frame. Do some research previous to your call to see who else they have coming in and perhaps suggest that you can open for a particular show you noticed on their upcoming schedule. Be nimble with another choice of dates for when you will be back in the area.

Second Call: If you do need to make the second call, which is often likely, then make sure you use your deadline at the start of the conversation to see if they are any closer to having an answer for you. Keep in mind, "no" is the second favorite answer of booking agents all over the world. When you get a "no," get information about other potential dates or programming opportunities. Best of all, you can now move on and make calls to other venues.

Third Call: If you are willing to give it three calls, then again, try to set a date closer than "next week" and reinforce your deadline. If they are no closer to an answer, let them know you are interested in working with them in the future and will be back in touch when you are booking dates in their area again, but you need to move on to fill this date. Thank them for their consideration. Sometimes, this alone may spark their interest to really look at the calendar and take you more seriously.

Biz Booster #57
Negotiation Technique: Playing for the Door—How to Make Sure Everyone Pays

Percentage gigs or playing for the door is often one way to break into a new market or play new venues.

Your biggest challenge is to get accurate audience counts when a door person is collecting the money, rather than a box office.

It's difficult for you to prepare for your show and keep tabs on the door. That is certainly true when it is a bar gig with multiple sets and people coming in throughout the night. The club or venue usually takes care of collecting the money with one of their employees, so whew you don't have to worry about that, or do you?

Yes, it's great that someone else is responsible, but the money collector doesn't work for you, they work for the venue. They have the venue's interests in mind and not necessarily yours. The money collector probably lives in town and may be familiar with a lot of the people who frequent the venue, whereas if you are a touring artist you may just be passing through.

So here are some problems to be aware of and some solutions to begin using on your very next percentage or door gig:

The Problems:

1. You neglect to discuss who collects and how the money is collected at the time you book the gig.
2. The money collector, if provided by the venue, may have friends that they let in for free. There goes some of your income.
3. They may only collect for the first part of the night and not the full night. This accounts for a bunch of lost income.
4. They may pocket some money—after all, who would know—and only report a fraction of the real income to the club owner.
5. They may report all the money to the club owner, but the club owner may only report a fraction of the income to you.

Some Solutions:

1. Include a discussion of money collection in all of your negotiations. Let the booker know that you have some ideas to discuss with them, in a non-confrontational manner, regarding the money collecting process.

2. Buy a *tally hand counter* either manual or electronic, ranging from $6.-$16. They have them at office supply stores or many online outlets, just Google "tally hand counter."

3. If you have not negotiated providing your own money collector then, get your own door monitor whose job is to stand next to the money collector and click the hand counter each time a person pays, and makes sure that all of the people are paying. Most of your travel entourage probably has their responsibilities laid out for them, so you might want to tap some of the following folks for this job.

   If you have a loyal friend, family member or fan in the town where you are playing, ask them to be your door monitor for the night or even to come to a number of local gigs in their area. You can offer to pay them with free tickets to the show, in CDs, in merchandise or even with an hourly wage. Believe me; they are worth their weight in gold! The difference you will see in your income will astound you. They can confirm that those on your comp list are the only ones let in for free. The counter numbers can confirm the exact number of paid people when you settle your money for the night.

   Ask to meet the money collector before the gig starts, introduce them to your counter person/door monitor so there are no questions, control issues or weirdness when people start coming in. They are now officially on notice that you are in charge and watching out for your business.

4. Make sure the money collector is collecting money at the door until one-half hour before the end of your last set. If you want to collect a lower ticket fee for the last set of the night, that should have been negotiated when you booked the date. Most venues stop collecting money much earlier in the night, resulting in less income for you.

These four steps, when done consistently, will increase your income on those playing-for-the-door gigs. Try it on your next percentage gig and track the results for yourself.

Biz Booster #58
Realistic Pricing

It all starts by establishing your value in the markets where you play. Whether you are an agent booking solos, duos, trios or any configuration of a group, or whether you are booking your own act, establishing the value of the act in the desired markets is the one true way in which you can begin to create realistic pricing.

It is not the number of people in the group or even necessarily the night of the week that matters. It is the perceived value of the act that drives the negotiation.

Let's test this. Take two solo performers, one new, emerging act and one, shall we say, Eric Clapton, performing solo. I think you get where I'm going with this. The value is in box office receipts and who can sell tickets.

If you are just beginning to build your act's reputation or value in a new market, you'll have less leverage to negotiate a good fee because your ticket-selling power is an unknown factor. So you go in with a percentage or a very low guarantee plus a percentage. You play the venue, do all you can do to get press, build a loyal fan base and get your foot in the door so you can come back a second and third time. If you do a great show and get some supportive press, your market value increases. Next time through you'll be able to leverage the success of the previous gig into a higher percentage and a higher guarantee.

Keep records of the number of tickets sold, the kind of press that was done, the type of email or social networking campaign that was done and the merchandise sold. Also keep track of any other events or type of weather that occurred on that day that might have influenced ticket sales.

It's all about the value that the venue booker perceives that the artist has in their market and in their venue. They are just as happy to have a hot selling artist on a Tuesday night whether they show up with a full band or play solo, as long as the venue booker sees evidence that the artist can sell tickets. If the artist has a track record of selling tickets in their venue and in venues throughout the region, then they will offer an appropriate fee. Work on building value, the money will follow.

Biz Booster #59
Negotiating Gig Fees

Let's get down to some basic truths about negotiating.

No two negotiations will be the same. You must approach each venue booker with the intention of building a long-lasting relationship based upon mutual needs in service to an appreciative audience.

Every negotiation has the potential for creative deal-making based on the individual situation. So get creative and examine all of the options open to you at the time. Perhaps you never asked for a percentage of the bar, they may not give it, but you'll never know until you ask. Just because you are used to getting a certain percentage of the door, doesn't mean you can't try something new.

Begin working with realistic budgets. You can never know how good the deal is, if you are not working off of a realistic tour budget. Creating a tour budget for each tour, no matter how short or long, will give you realistic starting points for each negotiation. It allows you to offer lower fees where appropriate, knowing that the high-paying nights still allow you to meet your budget over the course of the tour.

Use your numbers from your previous gig history in the venue or gigs in the region to promote your market value and leverage higher fees and peripheral benefits, like meal buyouts, housing, travel and advertising by the venue.

Listen to the offers and consider them before accepting, rejecting or making a counter offer. Always take some time to add a creative spin when making a counter offer if one is required.

There are no hard and fast rules about what fees will work across the board whether you are a solo, duo, trio or larger band. Look to build relationships that offer you greater opportunities to reach realistic gig fees based on the specific situation being negotiated.

There's so much more to this negotiation game. Please see my articles on negotiation at Performingbiz.com, (http://www.performingbiz.com/articles) for more details and read some of the many negotiation books available.

Biz Booster #60
Assume Nothing!

We get in trouble when we make assumptions. Like the time you assumed they would have four mics because you needed two vocals and two instrument mics, but they only had two. After all, you were only two people, they assumed you only needed two mics.

Or like the time you assumed the date was confirmed even though you didn't have a contract and you assumed someone sent it and it had been signed and returned, but wasn't.

So now would be a great time to stop assuming and take control of your situation with a set of planned strategies that insure things will be as you expect them to be.

Here are nine steps you can take right now to avoid making the wrong assumptions.

1. Send a contract for each gig as soon as you confirm the date. Even if it is just a letter confirming all the details you agreed on when you spoke.
2. Request a deposit of anywhere from 10%-50% on any gigs above $500.
3. Include a technical rider and a hospitality rider with each contract you send.
4. Include a request for media contacts, directions, housing information with each contract you send.
5. Include any marketing materials with each contract so that is taken care of and done.
6. Make sure you note the date that you expect the contract to be returned with any deposits. This date should be no longer than fourteen days from the day you sent it unless you specifically have discussed another scenario.
7. Call the venue immediately with any questions you have about the contract to clear up any inconsistencies. Do not wait!
8. Check with the venue's tech people to confirm that all of your technical requirements are being met many weeks before you leave for the date or the tour.
9. Commit to advancing each date in a timely, strategic manner to insure that every aspect of the date is being taken care of, from technical to hospitality, from ticket sales to marketing and promotion. Don't assume it is being done without checking that it is being done with the person responsible for each aspect.

By adopting an attitude of helpful cooperation, your consistent, strategic contact portrays you as a professional taking care of your business for everyone's benefit. Your attention to detail will be appreciated. Anything less, leaves you and the venue open to disappointment when either one assumes things are being taken care of.

Biz Booster #61
Negotiating Gigs—No is Just the Beginning

Rejection sucks! And when you are booking yourself, it's even harder to hear the booker say "No!" It just makes you want to take the rest of the day off.

Imagine this. You've spoken to the booker at least twice now. You really think you are developing a good rapport. You've been able to joke around a bit. He has taken your calls each time. He even told you how much he's enjoying your CD. Everything sounds really positive.

Now this is your third call, the one who said that he'll know something about the date you're discussing. And then, BAM! He tells you "It's a no-go." Your heart just sinks, your voice gets all small, you feel rejected and you get ready to hang up the phone with a very wimpy, "thank you."

But wait! There is another way this could go if you adopt the strategy that "No" is just the beginning.

When you get a "No," don't hang up, get information. When you get a "No," that's the time to start asking questions, begin a new conversation about a future date, future events and new possibilities. Remember, "No" is my second favorite answer when it comes to booking gigs. You know where you stand, you can now move on.

Now let's imagine that same phone call, only this time, instead of getting all depressed about losing the gig, you perk up, slap a smile on your face and fire right back, "Ok, so it won't work for you this time, but we'll be coming through again in a few months. Let's look at a date during July."

Or, how about asking, "What about the festival you've got coming up later this year? Perhaps we could do some workshops and perform during an early time slot? This could help build up our audience in the market for a date after the festival."

Or even, "I see you've got so-and-so playing next month. We'd be a perfect opener."

With these three new conversation openers, you've just moved on from the rejection and created some new opportunities. You're thinking on your feet and got them to start thinking of new ways they can fit you into their schedule. Plus you've extended the conversation and are now ending with positive new situations rather than on a negative note. This shows you off as a professional, willing to go with the flow and work with the booker to fit into their situations.

Next time you get a "No," don't hang up until you've begun a whole new conversation and created some new opportunities.

Biz Booster #62
Settling the Gig: Cash or Check?

Does your contract specify your preferred method of payment when settling your gigs? Do you let the booker know your preferences if you don't have a contract?

What is the best method of payment? This might seem a small point, but depending on the type of venues you normally perform in, this may be an issue deserving your consideration.

Now most artists performing at performing arts centers, on college campuses, for government organizations, in schools and sometimes at festivals, most often get paid by business check, government check or certified check. In some instances, money can even be paid into a paypal account or wired to your bank account.

If, however, you normally play nightclubs, clubs, house concerts and sometimes even sheds or are booked by a third party or a promoter, then cash is king.

That's right. *When you get paid, get cash*. It's not that the majority of these types of venues are going to rip you off, on the contrary, most will even offer to cash their own check right there and then. If you are offered the opportunity to have them cash their check, take it.

There are, those rare instances when a check just might bounce, so rather than taking the chance that this one out of a hundred venues, is the one where that occurs, make it your policy to ask for cash. From now on, put it in your contract, make it known when negotiating the gig. Be specific when settling the gig that you would like to get paid in cash. You want them to know in advance so they have the cash on hand. Then you remove any possibility of having a problem cashing the check.

If you've ever had a question about how to handle settling your gigs at clubs or with concert promoters, get used to asking for payment in cash. Now depending on the country in which you are performing, check the exchange rates for the best cash opportunity the day of your gig as well as prior to setting out on tour.

How you manage your finances on the road is something to plan long before the moment you settle your gig.

Networking

Biz Booster #63
Pull New Contacts from Old Contracts

Once a gig is played, the old contract gets filed away, hopefully. It's likely that you will get back to that venue's booker in a few weeks or months as you look for another date later that year or the next year. Instead of waiting for too much time to slip by, why not get back to the booker within days of the recently played gig and do four things.

1. Thank them for the past gig.
2. Mention a time-frame in the future when you plan on returning to the area and see if they will put a date on hold for you or actually book the date.
3. Ask them if they could refer you to three other venues, festivals or events in the region that won't interfere with your next gig at their venue, but that could help you build your audience in the area. This will further increase the turnout at their venue when you do return. Get a name and contact information and ask if you can use their name as a reference. Now, you have an in and it is no longer a cold call.
4. While you've got them on the phone, ask if they can give you a quote about your recent performance. You'll send them an email reminder to which they can easily reply.

You probably have plenty of old contracts filed away

somewhere. Why not pull them out, dust them off and sift through the contacts from previous dates played. You will have the history of the past gig to get the conversation rolling, whether you speak with the person you worked with at the time or a new person. The fact is, you played their venue, and you have history with that venue. Use these old contracts to drum up new gigs. It's like returning to old familiar ground with such great potential to add to a tour or set up a new anchor date.

Biz Booster #64
Tap Local Businesses for New Performance Opportunities

Make a list of businesses you know or do business with now or have done business with in the past. Many businesses have events for their employees that may be a possible performance opportunity for you.

Invite the other members of your group, friends and family and possibly some close fans to a brainstorming session to come up with a creative list of potential contacts from folks they know and do business with.

Start getting in touch with these contacts using the referral method to create a working list of potential new gigs. Once you've created a relationship with some local businesses, ask them for a referral to some of their friends in similar businesses in nearby towns or around the region. You'll be pleasantly surprised at the results.

Biz Booster #65
Use Your Mailing List & Fans for Referrals

Step 1: Start by adding a column to your mailing list or sign up sheet headed, "Occupation." Not only does this help you get to know your fans better, but it gives you a better idea of their socio-economic background, which can help you target your marketing more appropriately.

Step 2: Use this information wisely. Perhaps some of these fans work in positions that could help you get future gigs. Perhaps some can give you names to contacts at their business or organization who might be in a position to hire you for a performance event.

Step 3: Make that next referral call and mention your fan's name and their recommendation to call. Once again, because this is a referral, this call has much more potential to get a positive response.

Biz Booster #66
Identify and Use Your Unique
Niche Market's Networking Channels

If you have already discovered a unique niche market that is perfectly suited to your performance, congratulations! If not, here are five suggestions to put this valuable asset to use in turning cold calls into referral calls. If your niche market is an organization with multiple chapters or offices that spread across a state, a region or is national or international, then you have hit the jackpot! Now let's get to work utilizing all of the amazing benefits offered by your association with this niche.

Get in touch with the contact at the niche with whom you have worked before.

1. Ask them for a letter of reference or a quote about the last show you did for them, if you haven't done this already.
2. Ask if they have a list of other chapters with a contact that they might share with you and if any of those on the list are personal contacts of theirs that they could refer you to directly. Don't forget to ask if you could use their name.

3. Ask if there are any chapter-wide events coming up, such as meetings or conferences, where you could perform, or give a workshop and showcase your act to a larger portion of the chapter's membership and potential programmers for future events.
4. Ask if there is an organization-wide newsletter where an article about your group's involvement with this organization might appear.
5. Ask if the newsletter or website offers any advertising opportunities. Often these ads are much less expensive and are a direct link to a large and enthusiastic membership if you've chosen the right niche.

Referrals from within a niche market have a high degree of credibility among niche members often resulting in a domino effect. Once one chapter discovers you and has a successful experience with your act, the referrals become almost automatic and spread like a virus throughout the niche market, thus expanding your reputation as well as the number of gig requests. Making your calls by referral within the niche, becomes a series of pleasant conversations with people who are eager to speak with you and welcome your call, if they haven't called you first.

Rely on all the connections you have made over the years. They can provide you with a gold mine of potential new venues to play, turning those dreaded cold calls into more pleasant referral calls, paving the way to more successful bookings.

Promotion & Marketing

Biz Booster #67
When are Your Marketing
Materials Good Enough?

The first thing you have to realize about creating great marketing materials, is that it is an evolutionary process. Your materials need to capture where you are currently in your career and express those facts concisely and powerfully. The information also needs to be easily accessible to your specific audience.

Ask yourself the following questions as you review all of your marketing materials, EPKs, websites, press releases, one-sheets, CD covers and inserts:

1. Does my material really reflect who I am as an artist now?
2. Have I told them who I am and what I do right away, or do they have to search for that information?
3. Have I conveyed through words, images and sound, my unique selling points as an artist, to help my audience distinguish how I differ from others in my genre or field?
4. Is it easy for my potential customers, fans, or media contacts to understand immediately what I offer through my art?
5. Have I presented my materials in an organized fashion so that someone searching for specific information can access it and use it easily? Is my stuff user-friendly?

With marketing materials, there is no such thing as good enough. There is, however the *right* marketing tool for the right occasion. Creating specific materials for a variety of situations should be your goal so that you may connect more precisely with your targeted audience whether it is your fans, your booking prospects, your media contacts or your potential industry partners.

As the need changes, your marketing materials should adapt. As your career evolves, your marketing materials need to capture your growth and express your new career development. Be proud of the materials you create for the specific situations if they succeed in the task for which they were created. Tweak and revamp your materials as necessary when they don't fulfill your expectations. Be very critical of your materials if they don't satisfy your intended goal before you invest in their long term use as your representative to the world.

Biz Booster #68
Writing the Right Press Release
for the Right Audience

Writing a press release for an intended audience is not a one size fits all, scenario. If you want to broaden your outreach, you may need to narrow your focus and write more directly to your various audiences.

Start with a basic press release that covers the main information you want to get across. This may be as short as a three or four sentence, second paragraph. The first and last paragraph will normally include the, who, what, where, when, why and how of the press release.

Here are three ideas to help you write a press release that really speaks to your intended audience:

1. Identify the various audiences you are attempting to reach. This may include a list of the various types of

media outlets, newsletters, organizations, fans and business people.

2. Separate this list into categories. For example: general public media, niche organizations with similar interests, fans from specific niches such as churches, charities, schools, business associates with specific functions who impact your career such as booking personnel, conference organizers, labels or industry executives.

3. Review your basic press release and with each of these categories of intended recipients in mind, tweak the basic press release to address the readers in that category. You may need to add a sentence or change the tone of the press release or highlight something that would specifically interest members of that category.

Knowing and understanding who your audience is, is the crucial difference in how your press release is received, used and ultimately reacted to by the end reader. Does the writing reach the intended audience and cause them to act in the manner you intend?

If you have a general press release on hand, look it over and for your next project, performance date, release or event, consider tweaking your press release to write specifically to the intended audience. It may mean that you send out three different press releases or even more.

Then measure your results to see the responses. Each time, you may need to tweak it a bit more or really change it to fit the reader; but over time and with practice, you will have more media insertions, more responses, more additions to program copy, get more reviews and interviews and ultimately, more ticket sales for your shows.

Biz Booster #69
How to Become Newsworthy

What is newsworthy to you may just not be newsworthy to the editor, the program director, or the producer. They are looking for items that will interest the largest segment of their readers, listeners or viewers. Or, they are looking for items that will interest an important niche segment of their customer base.

You must begin viewing your communications to the media from their perspective.

Here's an example that may be near and dear to you, a CD release. This is of course great news to you and something that is very important to your career. But, to the media, it is another CD release among many.

What is unique about this release? Now this is certainly something you might consider before you even start thinking about doing the next CD. How can your marketing campaign for this new CD be more newsworthy?

Newsworthy means it has an impact beyond your own income and business well-being. It impacts your local community or the greater world community. It may involve community organizations, businesses, charities, schools or well-known community members.

If you are not already a household name in the entertainment world, then your CD release may not be newsworthy. Unless the local or national media you are trying to reach specifically serves its community with CD reviews, such as Billboard Magazine, you need to be more thoughtful about creating newsworthy communications with your media contacts, so you can gain broader coverage.

Here's a practice exercise: Pretend or use a real CD release situation and write a press release.

First, make a list of a few ways in which your CD

can have an impact on the larger community. Maybe you have a relationship with a local or national charity or organization or cause or event. Perhaps a song on the CD has a specific message that can be used as a news item. Perhaps there is a theme, like the environment, business, kids, or maybe you partnered with some organization to release the CD and it partially benefits that organization. Dig deep and come up with something beyond the CD release itself.

Now write the press release with the lead being about the point of interest, the organization, the charity, the cause partnership. In the later paragraphs you can talk more about the CD details, the musicians and yes, even yourself. First, make it about the unique collaboration or item of interest. Now you are beginning to create something to which the media can wrap their headlines around and dedicate extra print space or air time.

When you plan ahead and think from the media's perspective, you have a much better chance of getting more coverage for your events and projects.

Biz Booster #70
You've Got Thirty Seconds to Hook Them

What's your elevator speech? Whether you are actually on an elevator at a conference or on the phone trying to book a gig, those first thirty seconds of introduction can make or break the rest of the conversation.

So how do you introduce yourself? Are you creating some intrigue with your introduction to make your listener want to know more about you? Examine the introductions that you use when making booking calls or when you are in a networking situation. Listen to yourself and if you can, write down your intro so you can examine your words more carefully.

1. Are you including at least one interesting fact?
2. Have you chosen descriptive words that are unique?
3. Is your intro brief and to the point or long and wordy?
4. Can you find information buried in your bio that ought to be included or brought to the forefront of your introduction?

When you examine your introduction and then revamp it, try it out on friends, family or other artists and perhaps even a few friends who might also be in the position to book you. Gage their response. Do they ask you more questions and want to engage in a deeper conversation or is there silence?

Make your introductions more interesting so you may develop more engaging business relationships. Remember, entertaining does not just occur when you are on stage. You need to bring your full personality to the forefront whether you are on the phone booking a date or meeting someone after a workshop at a conference or Tweeting someone you just met on Twitter. Be engaging, be interesting and unique. It may all start with how you introduce yourself for the first time. You've only got thirty seconds to capture their attention. Make it count!

Biz Booster #71
Fit Your Message to Your Market

Why won't those bookers reply to your emails? Why can't you get an interview scheduled with the local newspaper? Why aren't your fans buying your CDs from your website?

Maybe your message just isn't hitting a home run with your audience. I'd like you to really think about your various markets or audiences. When you take a close look at all the people to whom you might be marketing, it will become very clear that you have at least three specific and different audiences, if not more.

Spend some time identifying each of your different audiences so you may begin creating audience-specific messages that will help you communicate more effectively with each one. Make a list of appropriate words that work with each individual audience group.

First there are your fans. You talk to your fans differently than you would talk to a venue booker or a media person.

Next you have the folks that book you. This group may need to be divided further because not all venues are alike. In this group you may have festivals, clubs, performing art centers, corporate and charitable organizations, house concerts and private events, schools—universities, elementary and high schools. You may also work in other arenas such as on cruise ships or at dinner theaters. As you can see from this list already, you have quite a number of separate groups that you may be lumping together as "your audience."

Finally, there is the media. This audience group ought to also be further divided into smaller groups such as print, radio, TV and Internet. Each of these groups will require their own unique communications if you want to be truly effective with all of your marketing.

What I am suggesting here, is that these various audiences need to be thought of and communicated with as separate entities requiring their own unique communications. With the above suggestions in mind, create your own lists specific to your act and the kinds of venues in which you perform and the types of media outlets you generally use to promote your performances.

The next tip will help you focus on the words you use to correspond to your separate audience types.

Biz Booster #72
Words that Get Replies

You sent the email, but, no one replied. It may be the way you are communicating with your audience. More specifically, it could be the words you are using to put your message across.

Now that you have identified all of your various audience types from above, let's make all of your future correspondences more targeted by choosing your words to create messages that are specific to your various audience types. For instance, if you are trying to book college gigs, you may be dealing with a student organization that has an advisor. You may be working with the head of a specific department trying to book a master-class rather than a workshop. When booking a festival, you would use the term workshop rather than master-class.

If you work in elementary schools you could be communicating with a principal, a teacher or a district supervisor or a Parent Teacher Organization, PTO or PTA and you would be talking about residencies or assembly programs rather than concerts.

Perhaps you book performing arts centers where you'll most likely work with a presenter rather than a booker as you would in a club. You will also work with an artistic or program director at a festival rather than an event planner as in corporate or wedding scenarios.

Right from the start, addressing the appropriate person, helps target your message more efficiently. Then, using appropriate terminology for each situation lets the recipient know that you understand the people with whom you are communicating.

You would do well to spend a little time getting to know each of your specific audiences, so that you may incorporate the language of your target audience into each of your messages.

One of my favorite examples is about one of the bands in my home town. A few years ago, Bella Morte, a Goth band, was trying to get a loan from a local bank to produce and market their next CD. They prepared a full Power Point presentation with sales figures, marketing budgets, point-of-sale descriptions and numbers from stage, Internet and mail order. They went into this meeting dressed in their stage costumes, but, proceeded to speak the language of bankers: numbers, numbers and numbers. Their presentation described exactly how they intended to pay back this loan based on audience ticket sale history, future bookings, touring budgets and historic sales figures. They got the loan on the spot. Why? Because they spoke the language the loan officers understood.

If you want to communicate more effectively with your various audiences, learn their language and use the appropriate words and phrases.

Biz Booster #73
Get to the Main Point—Fast

In order to get your messages read and acted upon, you must decide what the main point of every message is, and put it up front.

I read tons of bios, web sites, press releases, email campaigns, newsletters, blog posts, letters of introduction, proposals and, well, you name it. Most writers have trouble identifying their main message and then once they stumble upon the main point, it gets buried in the third or fourth paragraph.

Everything you write on behalf of your act deserves consideration and attention to determine what is it that you are asking of the reader. I believe there are two main things to consider.

1. What information do you want them to get from this message?
2. What action do you want them to take after reading this message?

I also think it would help you, when crafting your message, to fit the message into a category.

Here are four categories that would fit your specific needs.

1. Booking
2. Marketing
3. Selling merchandise
4. Disseminating general information

Once you determine which category your message fits into, it is much easier to get to the point of your message.

As an example:

If you are writing an email campaign to get bookings, then put that point up front, come right out and state your intent rather than beating around the bush or mixing your message with other non-related items. State your intent and then build your case around your main message.

If you want a reviewer to review a new recording, ask them up front. Then tell them why they should review it by sharing information about the recording, the players and the production.

When you bury the main point, you have a greater chance of causing the reader to lose interest before they discover the main point. From now on, make your messages count by thinking about the main point of each message and then feature it up front. Support your main point with valuable information to continue to build your case for what you are asking of the reader.

You will find your readers are much more receptive to your messages and your messages are shorter, less confusing, more focused and more successful.

Biz Booster #74
What Programs Do You Offer?

Have you made it clear what programs you offer? Does your website, marketing material or even letters to potential bookers, make it clear what kinds of programs, concerts, workshops or events you present?

I know this may seem like a silly question to focus on, but I visit so many artists' websites and it is not clear what they are offering. If it's not clear, then how do you expect a booker to book you or a school concert committee to know what they are getting into? I mostly see this on musician sites. Theater artists are generally focusing their information around a specific show or season of shows, but musicians tend to think that anyone visiting their site assumes they play concerts.

That's fine, yes you play music, but, if you would take some time to think about the various ways in which you like to present your concerts or workshops or the multiple configurations in which you might perform, you just might create some clear options to offer your venues and event bookers. When bookers have clear options, they make faster choices. If your offerings are more descriptive and interesting, they may choose you over the hundreds of other artists who haven't taken the time to create and describe their performance options. This is particularly important if you also present workshops or can do a master-class.

When you break down your performance options and create multiple opportunities for a presenter to offer to their audience, you create multiple income streams for yourself.

Take some time and review your website to see whether you have clearly defined your performance offerings. Think about your concerts. Can they be broken down into a variety of programs based on themes, or topics? Give them cool names and vivid descriptions. Then drive your presenters to that page so they get clarity on what it is that you are offering their audience.

Have fun with this, make it interesting. It could just be the ticket that gets those bookers and presenters to book you rather than someone else.

Biz Booster #75
Uniquify Yourself

Are you following the crowd? Trying to play at all the places the other artists you know are playing?

Now, it is more important than ever, to call attention to yourself and your art by standing out from the crowd. That is why it is so important to find your unique qualities and promote them.

In the search for acceptance, so many artists try to be like the artists who everyone already knows and likes. But that artist became known and liked because they stood out from the rest.

What makes you stand above the fray? What quirks, physical attributes, vocal qualities, instrumental prowess or personality differences help make you the artist you are? Are you incorporating those aspects of yourself into your biography, upfront and not buried in the third or forth paragraph?

Audiences, fans and industry professionals look for something new, something unique to connect with all the time. Can you give them that?

Take a really good look at yourself and your act and consider how you may be able to *uniquify* yourself. Find that one quality you may have wanted to hide in the past thinking no one would like that about you or you might have been embarrassed to show or be or write about. Audiences want to see something interesting, be a part of something new and exciting. The media is looking for something exciting to share with their audiences. Same old, same old just doesn't cut it. So find your unique qualities and talk about them, let them shine, let them propel you above the crowds of other performers. Get interesting, *uniquify* yourself!

Touring Strategies

Biz Booster #76
Diversify Your Performance Venues

Are you focusing your bookings on only one type of performance venue? Perhaps you play clubs or festivals or soft-seat theaters exclusively. You may be limiting your performance opportunities by doing this.

Here are some alternative booking ideas you may want to incorporate into your booking plans.

House concerts or private events: Try dipping into your own mailing list for possible gigs here. They may be excited to offer you a gig to introduce you to their friends, neighbors or relatives or their business associates. Holiday seasons are perfect for bookings at businesses.

College master-classes for specific departments: Don't limit yourself to the music department. You may write songs with specific themes that could be of interest to the history, journalism, economics, religion, English, science, dance, theater departments or departments of other ethnic cultures. You may just be able to do a workshop and concert for a captive and attentive audience. If you haven't already created a master-class or workshop, think about all you have to offer and begin developing one.

Local area events: Look for museums, wineries, local and town government parks and recreation concert series. Not only are there potential great paying gigs available, but, these public performances are a fantastic way to expand your audience and develop new and loyal fans.

Diversify the types of venues you pursue and you will expand your opportunities for new gigs, grow your audience and possibly increase your gig fees.

Biz Booster #77
Booking Around Anchor Dates

What is an anchor date? It's general the main date or the first date booked in a tour. Often these may be booked far in advance. They may pose a challenge when making a commitment so far out, especially if it's a distance away with a low performance fee. Anchor dates booked in the distance make sense when they pay enough money, so in case you can't really make a tour out of it, it can stand alone as a date and you'll still come out ahead.

Here are some tips to help turn your anchor dates into a tour.

When you make your commitment to the date, make it contingent upon getting a few more dates in the area. Give the contingency a deadline. For example, if, by "such and such" a date I can't get three more dates in the area, we won't be able to do the date or we will do it as a stand alone date for the full fee.

Ask the anchor date booker to refer you to three other venues in their region that won't interfere with their date, but that will help make their date possible.

Give that booking person some incentive such as offering a "Block-Booking Discount," if they help you get a few other dates in the area by actively referring you to the other venues. This means they give them a call on your behalf and suggest that if they come on board with another date you all get a discount on the fee.

If you have any fans in the region or even *en route* to the anchor date, send them a direct email and ask them for referrals to venues they know about in their town. Suggest to them that you are traveling through, and perhaps they would like to host a private event or house concert while you are in the area.

By using Biz Booster #75, you may be able to find alternative venues in the area surrounding the anchor date and fill in weekdays with master-classes, concert/lectures or private events for businesses in the area.

Having an anchor date booked in the future adds momentum and vision to your bookings. It gives you something to help leverage other bookings to expand your tour. Use these anchor dates as incentive for other bookers to jump onboard and be a part of a tour while you are in their area. It helps you increase your income for each tour and offers bookers potentially lower fees for each individual date. This is a winning situation for everyone.

Biz Booster #78
Regional Touring: Necessity or Missed Opportunities

With higher gas prices impacting tours to untried markets, it's time to turn your attention to performance opportunities closer to your home region. I've long been an advocate of creating a home base of support and expanding outward from that point. Now, more than ever, developing your local region more thoroughly is not only more cost-effective, but may help you open new markets within your region that you might have missed when your sights were set half a country away.

Here are a few ideas to get you started touring regionally.

Research some regional booking conferences instead of planning to attend a national conference. More venue presenters and media representatives will be found closer to home to help with those shorter mileage tours. On the performing arts circuit, APAP, Association of Performing Arts Presenters (http://www.ArtsPresenters.org) has regional conferences for the west coast, east coast and mid-west regions. If you're interested in college bookings, NACA, the National Association of Campus Activities (http://www.NACA.org) has divided the country into smaller regions for even more convenient booking opportunities at colleges. And while we're talking about colleges, don't forget about the various academic departments such as music, theater, English or history that may have master-class workshop/concert opportunities to fill in those off-days. State and provincial arts councils, each have extensive listings of presenting networks that can expand your booking possibilities. An extensive and valuable online resource with over 36,000 venues listed in regional directories is the Indie Venue Bible by David Wimble. (http://www.indievenuebible.com/jeri).

Now for events happening within your region, check each county or city local events calendar online. Don't forget about your local arts or daily newspapers that usually include weekly calendar listings of events. Make notes of events that are yearly occurrences, often free to the public and reach a large general audience.

As you ponder your local scene for performance opportunities, think beyond the night clubs and concert halls. Museums, aquariums, libraries and wineries often have concert series' throughout the year or at specific times of the year.

Private events and house concerts can also provide you with the means of developing a loyal following within your region.

Today's economic climate is forcing a regional booking strategy upon touring artists once again and I believe there are huge benefits to be gained to build a loyal fan-base, gain more media recognition and increase your income.

Biz Booster #79
Giving by Gigging

We all get more concerned with making donations around the holiday season, and that's a good thing. I encourage using your music to help community organizations with their fundraising. You can checkout my articles, "How You Can Give Back by Giving Your Music," (https://performingbiz.com/can-give-back-giving-music) or "How to Benefit from Playing Benefits," (https://performingbiz.com/benefiting-playing-benefits). Each article details ways that you can put your music to work for a cause. If you follow the steps laid out in the articles, you'll have a great foundation for finding appropriate organizations with causes you support. Now you can approach your organization, say a local food bank, Meals on Wheels, The Breast Cancer Fund, or any of those research organizations that constantly need financial support for the work they do, and make your proposal.

Here I'd like to offer some suggestions on how you might incorporate gigging for a cause throughout the year or for the duration of a single tour.

Contact your organization of choice and offer to donate a portion of income from gigs, CD sales and other merchandise sales over a specified time-frame, a tour, a month, a year. Be specific about the percentage. They need to have that for tax purposes and your fans and customers need to know for their taxes as well.

You might say $1 from each CD sold goes to The Breast Cancer Fund or you can use a percentage like 10% of all income from tour fees goes to the local Food Bank.

Once this is established and you have the blessings of the organization to use their name on your promotions, you may begin incorporating this information on posters, press releases, in radio interviews or even on your next CD pressing.

Now you have another newsworthy topic for the press to interview you about, to write about and help you sell yourself to bookers and potential ticket buying fans. But best of all, you are giving by gigging and using your talent, your music or performance for a higher purpose year round, not just during the holidays.

Biz Booster #80
The Best Weekend for Gigging in the U.S.

Have you booked your gigs for Thanksgiving Weekend yet? Whatever time of year you may read this, it's not too soon to offer you this booking Hot Tip.

It has been proven that Thanksgiving Weekend is probably the best Friday and Saturday night of the year for gigging. So I wanted to just remind you to start looking around for an appropriate type of gig for yourself on one or both of those nights. Why is it the best weekend? Just think about it. Whether people travel from their home to visit friends or family in another town, or people stay at home in their own town, everyone is probably itching to get out of the house and away from the leftovers by Friday night. What better way to take advantage of people needing to escape to something fun and different, than by offering a house concert, or a performance at a local venue. Believe me, many artists are already on the schedule, so why not you and why not this year?

If you have not already discovered this gem of a gigging weekend, I'd suggest you give it some attention as you consider where you might be this coming Thanksgiving.

Perhaps you'll be visiting friends and family. Ask them if they want to put on a house concert and invite all the neighbors who are probably also going to be thrilled to get out of their house for the evening. Or, call those you might visit and ask them about local venues, radio stations or local promoters in the area. Then get on the web and do some research, see whether they are booked. If they are, maybe you could open and begin building a following in the area. If they are not booked, great!

It's never too late to get a few extra fall gigs that are bound to be some of your best. Turn your holiday and those that come to see you into some of the best gigging nights of the year.

Biz Booster #81
The Worst Dates to Book Gigs

The truth is, there are just some dates that are terrible gig dates. There are only a few, but they are definitely dates to work around.

There are the logical holiday dates like Christmas Eve and Christmas Day and New Years Day. Easter Sunday is probably one to stay away from as well.

But the dates I want to discuss may change around the world depending on where you tour. The factor influencing these undesirable dates is major sporting events that command the attention of a large population. Even if you are not a sports fan, or don't pay attention to sports broadcasts, if it is either of these following events, odds are that a good deal of your audience is involved in some way.

For much of the U.S., the #1, major date to avoid is Super Bowl Sunday. So many people have Super Bowl parties, even if they don't care about the game, someone in the family does, so it becomes a party for everyone.

Sunday may not be a great date or night to perform in most cases anyway, but this one is one to avoid.

In Europe, South America and many other countries as well as the U.S., the World Cup Soccer Tournament is the big event.

No other sporting events really command as much attention as those two events, not even opening night of the Olympics. Sure you have the avid fans and followers of other types of sports and tournaments, but these are the ones that can capture the attention of whole populations whether they follow the sport or not.

I bring this to your attention, because as a performer, these types of events may not be at the forefront of matters you take into consideration as you plan your bookings. But I thought I would throw it out there so you can put it into your mix as you plan your tours. I also want you to become aware of all the factors that might influence your bookings. Be proactive when booking around these dates so you don't wonder where the audience was on one of those nights, you'll know. By planning ahead, you may be partying with everyone else instead of losing money on a bad gig night.

Biz Booster #82
Building Mid-Week Booking Momentum

How do you find a balance between a band's booking strategy to book dates far into the future and a venue's booking strategy to book closer to the play-date. Some clubs like to hold dates and wait to see what acts might be coming through.

There are two potential strategies that can help with this dilemma. The first suggestion is to look at mid-week and early weekdays as potentially optimum dates. As you do your research of venue calendars, pay particular attention to days like Monday through Wednesday. These days are often left either, unfilled, used for local or regional acts or are saved for national touring acts that might be heading to another market and happen to have an off-night.

These are choice nights to line up recurring gigs that can offer the venue a potential audience that they might not otherwise get, especially if you have a great following. The Dave Matthews Band played a regular Tuesday night gig at a local club here in Charlottesville, VA as they were getting started. It launched a flurry of media attention and built a feverish fan base.

By proposing an early or mid-week night, you offer the venue an opportunity for potential bar sales on an otherwise slow night. You also let them know that you are not looking to hog a weekend night when they normally make their big bucks, in case your fans don't show. This is a good relationship-building tactic.

The second strategy is to put a hold on a date they might be saving for an as-yet-to-be-booked act and suggest you would be available as an opener. Let them know you will be looking for other bookings for that night as well.

Then look for other gigs that you can lock in. If you book a solid date, then get back to the venue with the current hold, let them know you have been booked into another venue and they can remove the hold. You'll get back to them about a future date and thank them. This builds a good "buzz" with the venue booker as it shows them you are playing and other venues are booking you. It's also a great time to talk about future dates and perhaps next time around, they may be more likely to confirm their date with you rather than let another venue grab you first, again.

This strategy puts you in more control and builds a positive relationship with the booker because you were professional and got back to them. It builds your market value in the booker's mind—a very good thing.

Biz Booster #83
Holding Dates

What does it mean when a venue wants to put a hold on a date?

A hold can be a good thing. When a venue wants you to hold a date for them, they pencil you in on their calendar. Now they may have some reasons for not confirming the date with you right away. Some of those reasons may be:

1. They are waiting for confirmation from another act.
2. They are waiting to see if a bigger and more well-known act might be coming through.
3. They may need to check on facility availability.
4. They may need to wait for a grant or a funding cycle to begin, if they are a non-profit organization.

The three most important things that you need to do when a venue requests a hold on a date, are:

1. Get a reason for the hold.
2. Determine a deadline that releases you from the hold so you may look for other gigs in case this doesn't work out. Pick a deadline that gives you enough time to book a gig while taking into consideration their concerns.
3. Get something in writing from the venue that verifies that the date is on hold until notified that it is firm or not going to happen or until the deadline is reached.

Now as you scout for gigs, you may want the venue to place a hold on a date you are going after. Perhaps you are doing a tour through a specific market and that venue is a key date in your tour plans. The venue is not convinced you are right for that night, but they are willing to place a hold on the date for you. The same list from above applies in this case as well. So be persistent and make sure you check back often in either case to finalize the gig or move on to find another.

If the hold doesn't get confirmed this time, at least you were close. Maybe next time you'll get a contract.

Biz Booster #84
Book More Efficient Tours

Are you zig-zagging around your region or worse yet, around your country? Do you put more dollars in your gas tank than in your pocket?

Perhaps you need to create more efficient touring patterns by booking better routed tours. How do you begin to do that?

Concentrate on building your solid fan base regionally before hop-scotching long distances to open new markets. Work outward from your central base of support. As you move to new towns nearby, your fans are more likely to follow or may have friends or family in those nearby towns who they could tell about your upcoming gig.

Build upon media contacts that you've already developed by asking them who their contacts are in nearby towns. When you make that call, you can mention their name and get your foot in the door more easily and perhaps make a review more likely.

Look for multiple gig opportunities in each town to make travel distances much shorter between gigs. Back up those gigs with multiple media and promotional opportunities to reach different audiences in the same community.

When you take a regional approach to build a loyal and solid following, you can create tighter tours, save a ton of money on travel expenses and begin to leverage each gig to help book the next gig. Your fans may not choose to follow you many states, counties or provinces away, but they will follow you to a neighboring town. You'll begin to sell out your dates. You'll sell more merchandise and build a bigger buzz.

Biz Booster #85
Book Multiple Gigs in One Town

It always helps the bottom line when you can maximize your travel dollars. Here are some ideas on how to do just that by turning one gig in one town into multiple gigs in one town.

Perhaps you know of a venue in town you would either like to play or you already have a gig there. Start by doing a little research about the town. Check the local websites for the town and the Chamber of Commerce to get some idea of what else is in the town. Look for schools, colleges, businesses and organizations. Also, look for any locally sponsored events like fairs and festivals.

Depending on the time of year you are planning to play that town, research the schools and colleges if it's during the semester or research the fairs, festivals and other outdoor events if it's during the warmer months of year.

The benefit of playing an elementary school or even a college gig means that it likely won't interfere with the anchor date at the other venue.

If you are unable to line up a mainstream gig at a club or concert venue, then focus attention on your mailing list in the area and try to line up multiple house concerts within the same town.

The great benefit of doing private events and house concerts for your personal fans, is that it is unlikely that having two, three or even four house concerts in one town will ever overlap fans, since each fan has their own friends and family. So instead of playing a gig for two to six people at a club on a Saturday night, you might be able to turn a potentially bad gig into a multi-night stay and play for twenty people or more at each house concert.

Tap your fans for info about every gig you have booked right now and see if they can share some valuable background about their town. Use your fans to do some research for you and begin to extend your tours by multiplying your tour dates, one town at a time.

Biz Booster #86
Getting Your Foot in the Door

How do you get your foot in the door at new venues and get the booker to give you that first listen?

This fits nicely into a theme I've recently been discussing about creating touring patterns and why building that elusive "buzz" regionally is so important. Here are a few ideas to begin incorporating into your booking process.

When beginning to expand further out into your region, make it a habit of inviting the bookers at the venues you want to play, to come see you at a gig you are already playing. It's quite unlikely they'll take you up on the invite, but that doesn't matter. What this does is begin to establish, in their minds, that you are working at venues they heard about and perhaps even know the booker of that venue. So you start building a relationship without even asking them for a gig. They get to recognize your name and most importantly they see that you are playing. This also works with festivals.

Find a band you know who is playing at the venue you want to play and work out a gig swap with the band to have them invite you to open for them at their gig and you in turn, have them open for you at one of your gigs. This introduces each of you to a new audience as well as the venue booker you are trying to interest in your act.

If you have any friends or fans in the towns where you want to play, ask them to call the venue asking,

"When are they planning on having your group?" When the ticket-buying public begins to demand an artist, then the bookers take notice. So get on your social network sites and build your fan base in markets you want to play. Then nurture those fans to help create a demand for your act in their towns.

Venue bookers are highly motivated to take a chance on a new act when they get referrals from other bookers who have had the act, when fans are clamoring to hear an act and when the media is writing cool things about an act. Build your buzz so when you call or email or send material, your reputation has preceded you. They will return your calls and give you a shot at that point. There needs to be a perceived market value in order for a booker to invest in an un-tested act.

With so many acts to choose from, in this economy, they are mostly going to stick with acts that they know will bring in their fans and sell tickets. Give these strategies a try next time you are targeting a new venue.

Biz Booster #87
Use Recurring Events as Anchor Dates

I've talked about how to use anchor dates to move your bookings forward previously. Now I'd like to offer some ideas about how to use recurring events as an anchor date around which to plan a tour.

For example, take New Year's Eve Celebrations. It is a recurring event that you can plan on every year. Someone, some organization, some fraternity or sorority, some business is having some sort of party somewhere. How can you plan in advance, for the multitude of potential performance opportunities that will occur?

Start by paying attention to any media announcements about public events that are advertised or promoted this year such as conferences, fairs, festivals, special holiday celebrations, fireworks displays, etc. Look around your home town and make a list of any and all events in local papers, newsletters or that are announced on radio or TV. Note the presenting organization. Then as soon as the event is over, contact the event organizer to find out how you might be considered for next year's event. If the organizer promotes other events throughout the year, this would also be a great time to ask about those events and throw your hat into the ring for consideration.

Next, send a specific email to your own fan base asking if anyone is organizing an event for the occasion or if they might consider doing something and have you as the entertainment. If they are not personally planning something, then ask them if their business or organization might have planned something this year and could they refer you to the organizer.

Once you have an anchor date planned around a specific recurring event, you can build other dates around it on a regular basis. This might fit in perfectly with your touring pattern if you plan your tours to specific regions at specific times of the year.

Use special events or occasions to spark interest with potential organizations, businesses, venues or individuals. By calling about the specific event occurring at the time, you have a talking point of particular interest to help move your conversation along. It just might lead to other events at other times as well.

Biz Booster #88
Danger: Playing Too Much?

Are you in danger of playing too much in your chosen markets? We all want to gig more often, but have you really taken a look at how gigging too much in any given market might impact your ability to grow in that market? How can this be?

What are the effects of overplaying your markets?

1. Your audience dwindles
2. Your pay never increases
3. You can't get prestigious gigs
4. You are covered in the media less often
5. Your CD or merchandise sales slump

How can you avoid this unappetizing scenario? You've got to do three important things:

1. Keep track of your numbers: By tracking your sales, your audience counts and the size of the venues you are playing, you can see how much you are growing. You can determine, by these numbers, when it is time to stop playing once a week and start playing once a month to increase the demand rather than overexpose the act to the same audience.
2. Follow strategic goals to plot your growth in any given market: If you haven't set some growth goals, then there is no time like NOW to do this. As an example: Play once a week for six months at the same venue, then move to once a month, then once every three months and work this plan for two years as you increase your demand if the numbers are telling you that you have a growing following.
3. Accept fewer invitations to play benefits and be sure those you do play give you larger opportunities for audience and media exposure.

Look for private events and niche market events to round out your schedule to keep playing and open new audience segments in markets you already play.

Assess your current markets and evaluate the types of venues you currently play. Do they fit your career goals? If yes, then look for similar venues in nearby towns to expand your audience and build out regionally.

If the current venues are not ones you want to continue playing long-term, begin exploring smaller venues of the type you want to eventually play and make some contacts, attend conferences and perhaps showcase to start accessing your desired venue type.

Make small, strategic steps to plan your growth, build new audiences and make sure the number of dates you play does more to help you rather than harm you. Avoid the danger of playing too much, by planning exactly how much you should play as you develop your markets.

Biz Booster #89
Touring Preferences

It's really OK *not* to follow the crowd. So what if all the acts you know are playing at the club down the street. You don't like starting your gig at 11:00 p.m. And, if you play that club, you have to start at 11:00 p.m. If you don't play that club, then where are you going to play? That's the place you know about, so that must be the place you have to play, Right?

Wrong! You don't have to follow the crowd. In fact, you will do yourself and your art a great disservice if you do follow the crowd. If you are confused about where to set your performance venue targets, make a list of your performance preferences. You should have performance preferences to help you target your audience and your performance venues. Here's what to include on your list.

❖ Best times for your performance
❖ Best environment for your performance, dark smoke-filled bar, soft-seat theater, intimate coffeehouse, house concert, private event, large concert shed, library, school, festival, daytime event . . .
❖ Best stage setting for your performance

- Optimum age group
- Optimum ticket pricing
- Best method for customers to buy tickets, such as in advance, subscription series, through reservations, at the door, tipping, pass the hat
- Best time of year for you to tour
- Best climate for you in which to tour
- Best mode of travel for touring or playing single dates
- Best touring formats-solo, duo, trio, quartet, etc.
- Optimum amount of time to be on tour, solo dates, weekends, one week, two weeks, a month or more
- Optimum amount of time off between tour dates

Once you have your touring preferences list, you can immediately rule out certain types of venues, times of year, places and the way in which you are willing to do your tours.

Now you can begin to focus in on the prime venues or types of gigs that YOU want to play.

Believe me, once you can whittle down your options, you can be much more targeted, focused and strategic in planning your tours, accepting offers and zooming in to the best opportunities for you and your act. Take a few minutes this week and create your touring preferences list then update this list once a year since things may change along the way. It will serve you for your entire career.

Biz Booster #90
Advance Your Dates-Avoid Problems

Having a strategic plan to advance each tour date not only is a great way to keep in touch with your contracted venues, but more importantly, it is a way to protect yourself from potential problems. When you implement an ongoing template of follow-up with each contracted date, you are able to do some very important career building work.

For example:

- ❖ You build a deeper ongoing "working" relationship with the presenting organization
- ❖ You establish your professionalism
- ❖ You are able to get updates on their marketing and ticket sales
- ❖ You are able to answer the venue's concerns about any aspect of the upcoming gig
- ❖ You can help avoid potential problems with technical aspects of your performance
- ❖ You can step in to help with marketing in a timely manner should any of the venue's efforts fall short of your expectations and still make a difference in the turnout
- ❖ You can avoid consistent, annoying, ongoing questions from the venue when you are pro-actively engaging with them on your schedule

If you think that once you've got the contract in hand, the next time you need to contact the venue is when you are unloading your gear, then you may be in for some sad surprises.

Advancing your gigs is an art and tour managers around the world have perfected that art on behalf of their touring artists. Now you may not be ready for one of those top tour managers to join your team, but you certainly can take some tips from their playbook.

If you have my book, *How To Be Your Own Booking Agent,* (https://performingbiz.com/product/how-to-be-your-own-booking-agent) there is a Touring Checklist at the end of the very useful Chapter 10, "Managing the Road." If you have my Contract Forms Packet, (https://performingbiz.com/product/booking-contract-forms), the checklist is in there as well. If you are thinking of desig-nating someone in your group or on your team as the tour manager or the one to Advance the Gig, then this checklist would be very helpful to them.

However you do it, start to make a concerted effort to plan strategic check-ins with each upcoming gig. It will make a huge difference in your relationship with the venue, your media coverage and your income, not to mention your peace of mind, knowing exactly what you are expecting when you walk into the venue is exactly what you'll be getting.

Biz Booster #91
Maximize Your Opening-Act Slot

If you've landed an opening-act slot for either a single date or are lucky enough to be the support act for an entire tour, then here are some tips to help you maximize your opportunity. In other words-sell more CDs, endear yourself to the main act and their crew, win over a new audience and make a great impression on the venue's booking people, to land a gig of your own in the future.

1. Meet their road manager, band and crew, thank them for the opportunity and give them each a CD.
2. Ask the main act's road manager how much time they want you to play and then play only for that amount of time. Leave the audience wanting more, not begging you to get off the stage. This demonstrates courtesy to the main act and their audience. On stage, before you finish, thank the band, the venue and the audience for allowing you to share this time with them. Say something nice about the main act.
3. Make sure you know who is doing your sound. If it is the house sound crew, meet them and work with them. If it is the main act's sound crew, work with them and thank them. If it is your own sound crew, but you're using their sound reinforcement equip-

ment, be respectful.

4. If you get a sound check, and sometimes this is a big "IF," make sure you use only your allotted time and don't go over. If you don't like the final sound, but your time has run out, make that work for you and go have dinner.

5. Make sure you can sell CDs or other merchandise and sell them at the same price the main act is selling their merchandise. Sometimes openers don't get paid much, but they are able to keep most, if not 100% of the merchandise sales. Make sure your contract, if you have one, states any percentages due to the venue so you account for that in your sales price.

6. Meet the venue staff and give the house manager or stage manager and the booker CDs. Make sure you know who is paying you, the band or the venue and meet with that person in advance of the show to set a time when you'll get paid later.

7. Stay to see the main act's show. Don't leave before they finish unless they know you have another gig and you make your apologies before you play. Before you pack up and leave for the night, thank the band, their crew and the venue's crew. This might seem like a small, common sense thing to do, but you would be surprised how many artists forget this last thing. This is your last impression. Make it your priority, so you leave a good one.

Being an opening act is a lot of responsibility but it can open new doors, build new audiences and create some great new friends if you handle yourself well during the process. Be the act they want to have on their next tour and recommend you to their manager and agent. Be the act that the venue would like to book again. Be the act that the main act's audience would buy a ticket to see when you play in town. Follow these seven steps and you just might be that act.

Biz Booster #92
Opening New Touring Markets
Using Gig Directories

How can you effectively use gig directories to open new markets when you don't have any known contacts in those markets to help open doors for you? Here is a three step approach to break down the process.

Step One: *Review anchor dates already on the calendar.* As you look at any dates already set, whether they are performance dates, conferences, family or personal events, make a list of those dates that are in new markets where you have never played before and where you do not have any other connections in place.

Step two: *Ask yourself the following questions about each of those markets:*

1. Does this event afford me any time surrounding it to add performance opportunities?
2. Is this an area where I would like to begin building a fan base?
3. Does this market have media opportunities I'd like to access?
4. Have I heard of specific venues that I would like to play in the market?
5. Does this market fit into my overall artistic development goals?

Step Three: *Select appropriate markets.* Now that you have answered the above questions, you are better able to target the most appropriate markets to focus upon. Now you can finally turn to your directories. But which one will give you the most likely information without your sifting through thousands of possibilities? As you review the answers to the above questions, you can begin to pair down your options based on the following:

a. time
b. media
c. type of venue
d. career goals

For example: If you are trying to surround an anchor date that is coming up soon and you don't have much time to spend in the market, you may want to turn to a directory with club venues. Club venues don't book as far into the future as do performing arts centers. Club venues may have opening act slots more often than do performing arts centers. If, on the other hand, you have more lead time and more time surrounding the date, you may even want to access the Concerts In Your Home (http://www.concertsinyourhome.com) house concert database and see how you might fit a series of house concerts into your schedule. If you have at least twelve to eighteen months lead time, then you may want to search performing arts center directories for the area or even festival directories.

If you are not able to plug in performance dates due to the nature of how you are traveling or the type of event you are traveling to, you may want to simply access some radio and begin to establish a media presence in the market. In that case you can simply turn to a radio station directory.

When you create a profile of your needs based on your calendar, your use of gig and media directories becomes more focused, saves you time and effort and is much less overwhelming. You also begin to develop a pattern of gig research that is more likely to help you reach your career goals and build better tours. After all, isn't that what this is all about?

Biz Booster #93
The Santa Claus Theory of Booking

What if you knew what each of your prospective venue bookers wanted to book and it was in your power as a prospective act to give it to them? Wouldn't *YOUR* touring career take off?

So where does Old St. Nick come into this discussion? Let me share an example.

Remember when you were a kid and all you could think about was that shiny new toy you wanted for Christmas or whatever holiday you celebrated. You know the one, the red bike with the bell, the Barbie and Ken doll set, the signature baseball glove or that St. Louis slugger. And what happened when anyone in the family asked you that amazing question, "What would you like for Christmas?" You were bursting with excitement and blurted out your answer enthusiastically. And how many letters did you write to Santa asking for that special gift? Then on Christmas Day, there it was, like magic, under the tree. Was it a matter of mind-reading or a conscious clever effort of targeted questioning by family members to understand what's going on in your head?

Now let's transpose this example and put it to work on the booking process to get you some good gigs. Here's how my Santa Claus Theory of Booking works.

From the example above, we know that if we learned what the venue booker was looking for in an act, to fill their calendar, and we had that type of act, we could wrap it up in a pretty bow and hand it to them, right?

So get to know what they are looking for. In order to do that you need to know more about each of your prospective bookers, their venue, and their audience before you try to sell them your act. To do that, you need to build your relationship with that booker to understand them, their concerns, their booking goals and their tastes in talent.

You need to know what they are thinking about when they do their booking. Booking voodoo, you say! Santa's Theory of Booking, or just a savvy booking strategy that is more likely to get you the gigs you want.

In the next few Biz Boosters, I'll share some insights into each of your potential venue booking personnel's thought processes such as:

❖ Performing Arts Center Presenters
❖ Club Bookers
❖ Festival Artistic Directors
❖ College Student Activities Committees
❖ Elementary School Cultural Programming Staff

There are many others, but this covers a huge segment of the types of gigs you are after. By having a window into their booking thought process, you'll be able to frame your pitch more appropriately. I'll give you some ideas on how to do that as well.

Take a few minutes to make a list of all the types of venues you perform in now or would like to perform in, in the future.

Put my Santa Clause Theory of Booking to use on your bookings and wrap up your next touring season with a beautiful bulging bank account.

Biz Booster #94
Get Into the Minds of PAC Presenters

What are Performing Arts Center presenters thinking about as they consider which direction to take their programming season, year after year?

This entire process requires you to set aside your own goals for a bit and focus your attention on the needs, concerns and goals of the potential venue presenters with whom you want to work.

As you imagine swapping places with that person, you'll begin to understand their concerns. Here are just a few items on their list that will influence how they go about making booking decisions:

First and foremost is budget and funding sources. With constant cuts to federally funded programs for the arts and then cuts from statewide funding from the arts councils, presenters need to know that there is money to carry out any program they plan. They need to know they can pay staff as well as pay the artists they book.

Next, they must take into consideration the various membership programs they have. If they run a season subscriber series, they need to consider the kinds of programs that will entice their subscribers to renew their subscriptions. Donors will fall into this category as well and consideration is given to their preferences based on past contribution history.

The community factors into their planning also as they consider any community outreach or educational programming. Most of these types of programs are sponsorship opportunities for local businesses, so this gets factored in.

They also take into account when major tours are coming through the area, such as Broadway productions, symphony orchestras and operas. These often get locked into the calendar early, providing a framework for the season. These programs also claim a majority of the funding available but have the greatest chance to provide sell-out opportunities.

The presenter may also plan on seasonal programs for major holidays or calendar breaks in the school year. These may be of particular interest to you if you present a holiday-specific program.

Finally, the remainder of their season will be filled with artistic presentations the presenter feels is suitable for their audience, fits the remainder of their budget and has the greatest chance to sell tickets.

When attending booking conferences and presenter networking events, hot-button issues are discussed with other presenting organizations regionally and nationally. Presenters collaborate and consider booking acts collectively creating block-booking opportunities. Can you discover some of these issues and be part of the solution by attending these conferences?

By researching the venue, the community and the presenter, you may begin to piece together a booking pitch, when you fit their programming needs.

Framing your pitch can make or break your chances for consideration. I encourage you to look at your act, your performance and your program potential. What do you have to offer this presenter that may help them overcome some of their concerns? How can you frame your proposal to book your act in such a way, that it solves some of *their* problems instead of simply filling *your* calendar?

Ask questions about their goals and aspirations for their upcoming season. Ask how previous season programs were received by their audience and would they repeat similar programs in the future. Discover as much about them first, then, take some time to see how you can be a solution to their problems. When you present yourself in this manner, you will stand out from the crowd, you will become a valued artist under consideration. You will have a window into their mind and offer your act to help fulfill their programming goals while also meeting your own touring goals.

Biz Booster #95
Get Into the Minds of Club Bookers

Booking a club date is very different from booking performing arts centers. The folks that book clubs, work on a much shorter booking time frame, and have different concerns that drive their bookings.

A few years ago I wrote a column for *Gig Magazine* that was a series of interviews with club bookers across the country. My goal was to understand their thought process about how they selected their acts and what kind of marketing materials helped them make their choices. Here are some results from that research, along with insights from my own booking experience.

Clubs book on a short time frame, sometimes four weeks to two months out and often, if a hot act has an open date, the time frame may even be last minute. This makes it challenging for an act trying to do any long-term tour planning. Here is where a handy strategy of placing a hold on a date might be useful. It creates a relationship-building opportunity with the booker and forces you to keep in touch often.

Since many clubs have multiple shows each week, they need to make sure their "money nights," Thursday through Saturday, are winners. They use these nights to help pay their bills, so they are not willing to take a chance on an untested act on these nights. It doesn't necessarily have to be a national touring act, regional or local favorites are fine as long as they sell tickets, food and bring in healthy bar revenues. For many clubs, they make their money from the bar and possibly the food, so they are interested in getting a crowd, but are not wedded to the specific group. This sets up a dynamic, played out in so many clubs where the competition for gigs is at a fever pitch, driving performer fees down.

Filling the calendar in a timely manner to meet deadlines is also a driving force for the booker's schedule. You may find they are more non-committal and willing to "see who's coming through town" toward the beginning of the month and then set their dates rapidly as the calendar deadline approaches. But, if you wait until the later part of the month, you may just find them booked. Again, placing a hold on specific dates may prove to be a valuable tool.

Many clubs look to the week nights as a place to test new acts. If you have a growing following, you are more likely to get a favorable night and work your way into one of the "money nights."

Many club owners and bookers love to help develop new talent, especially when there is a glimmer of a bright future for the act to grow regionally and then nationally. Acts that fall into this category would be wise to discuss getting a regular night, multiple times a month to foster this audience-building process.

They want to know you have marketing tools and plans in place to help with any shows you do in the area. Most clubs do minimal marketing for individual acts. If you have a good mailing list and put it to use, that will be a plus for consideration. You have to leverage your pro-active marketing activities to help you stand out from the competition.

What can you do to make your act more attractive to the club booker?

Pay attention to any programs offered by the club for developing acts. Some have open-mic nights, others have a hierarchical method of developing talent by strategically placing new acts early in the evening and as their audience grows, moving them up to more prime-time night slots. Participate in these programs if you are new to the club.

Develop your audience fan-base in each new market and use your numbers of fans to leverage your value in each market. Club bookers appreciate a growing fan-base. To do this, use your social networks and email lists to nurture your fan-base. Make sure you share how many people on your list live in the area around the club. These numbers may mean more food and drinks sold along with tickets.

Track and share your numbers from past performances in the area. Remember how much merchandise you sold last time you came through town at this club or any others you've played.

Offer to arrive in town early to do radio interviews at appropriate stations or phone interviews prior to coming to town. Marketing for a club date is often left to the act. If you rely on the club for the majority of your marketing, you may be disappointed with the shared strip ad listing multiple acts for the month. Share your marketing plans with the booker to demonstrate your commitment to your audience development.

Make sure your set-up doesn't require any unnecessary expense or actions on behalf of the club or their technical staff. If you have unusual backline needs, make sure you carry those with you and are pro-active in creating an easy load-in, set-up and sound check.

Share marketing ideas that might create an interesting, unusual performance night. Any clever marketing pitch you can add to increase media attention or audience awareness, will work in your favor to build your value to the venue in that market.

Club bookers are juggling many more dates than performing arts centers. With a possibility for a different act six nights a week, it's likely you'll reach a club booker during a stressful time. Prepare your pitch, send appropriate materials that are easy to read and listen to and be prepared to make multiple calls to develop your relationship. Understand that when you meet with a harried voice on the other end of the phone, it's not about you, but the relentless pressure from the job. Be accommodating, plan your call-back time and be vigilant but not obnoxious. If you don't land your optimum date first time around, keep at it and plan for the next tour through the area. Remember, it's all about building the relationship.

Biz Booster #96
Get Into the Minds of Festival Directors

So, you would like to play some festivals? So far they've seemed pretty illusive. It would probably be a huge help if you began to think like a festival director. Since they have to knit together a cohesive, interesting, ticket-selling program, they are not just thinking about one act and how that act will sell. Instead, they are thinking about how to program multiple shows throughout the festival. They often start their creative process of thinking about the next year's festival while this year's festival is happening. They are constantly analyzing how the acts are working and how the audience is reacting.

If the festivals you are interested in playing also have workshop stages along with their performance stages, then you need to pay attention to this aspect of the festival. Here is where festival directors really show their creativity.

As you research each festival, review their most recent festival. Check out the previous year's acts. But, most of all, check the schedule, the way the festival is put together. See who followed whom and what titles were used for various workshops. This will give you the most insight into how the director thinks and plans.

Review the following for past festivals.

1. Workshop titles and the acts that are lined up in each workshop
2. Main stage and minor stage line-up

3. Side stage line-up, the stage that might have brief performances while the main stage is being set up for the next big act. If you are a novelty act that can perform two to ten minute sets, you might just be perfect on these stages and get to play in front of the main-stage audience multiple times throughout the main show.
4. Ease or difficulty of load-in and set up
5. The size of the act
6. The novelty of the act. Has the act been seen at other festivals before or is it new to the continent or country and is that of particular interest to the director?
7. Will the act be a draw or is the act just beginning to get known?
8. If the act is foreign, are immigration work permits a concern, a cost or a problem?
9. Will travel costs for any one act be a burden to the festival's budget?

When preparing your pitch to a festival director, plan to contact them no sooner than one month after the previous year's festival has ended. They need some down-time right after the festival. Here are some things you ought to be doing before contacting any festival director.

1. Review YOUR programs and what YOU can offer.
2. Do you have any workshops which you can moderate or be a participant?
3. Can you come up with some clever workshop names to suggest to the artistic director?
4. Do you have the potential to be used on a side stage during a main-stage change-over?
5. Are you willing to be flexible about the time of your performance? By offering your act for a day slot, you get your foot in the door, play the festival, develop your audience and the director's admiration and set yourself up for a more prime-time slot next year.

6. Have you built up enough of a following in the area to leverage your way into a showcase slot if one is offered? Sharing your statistics of audience development in the area can help with this.

Festivals are a great place for a new act to launch a new market, but you have got to be able to offer the artistic director some creative insights into who you are as an act and how YOU can help them create an exciting festival. Think about what they need to do and create your pitch with their needs in mind and you'll have a much better chance of playing the festivals you are itching to play.

Biz Booster #97
Get Into the Minds of College Activities Committees

Playing colleges can put some jingle in your pocket, but it's a true juggling act to complete a booking with college activities committees. Depending on which committee you are trying to work with, you need to prepare yourself for a different way of doing business.

You may be dealing with a student or student committee rather than a staff person. The Activities Director oversees the committee and will most likely be the person signing the actual contract, but it probably will be the students who make the booking decisions.

Since this is a college extra curricular activity for which the student contributes an annual fee, these programs offer entertainment or educational experiences to the student body. They have the money to spend and each committee MUST spend the money in order to be funded an equal or greater amount the next year. With this in mind, these student committees usually pay higher fees than, say, a club owner would since the committees are not necessarily concerned about their bottom line or needing to make money.

College activities committees look for novelty, they book concerts and coffeehouses according to what's in vogue, what's on the radio or what might be the next big-up-and-coming thing. Name recognition acts, popular mainstream acts are not necessary to sell to the college audience. These committees often take a chance on unknowns or "breaking" acts.

Since you will be dealing with students, having them make the deals and negotiate the contracts is part of their educational process, so you'll need to be somewhat, "educational" in your approach as well as patient. You are not dealing with a professional. They may not get back to you in a timely manner, they may even change positions and from one week to the next you might be dealing with a different student. Always make sure you know who the student advisor is for the committee. This will most often be the Student Activities Director.

Bookings often happen as a result of attending a campus activities booking conference, either a regional or a national conference as referenced in Biz Booster #25. When students attend these conferences they are inundated with the latest acts to hit the college market and do most of their booking with the acts or their agencies from the conferences. If you are attempting to break into the campus activity market, check out one of the regional conferences of these organizations and start your foray into college booking at the regional level to get acquainted with the scene.

Now when dealing with student committees, always get the student committee chair's name and supposed office hours, email and cell number so you can follow up with that student. If they haven't gotten back to you after a good first conversation where you were left with a positive impression of a booking, try the student advisor to get an update on the student's plans. Don't linger on the prospect of a booking if after three or four return calls to them, they are not getting back, move on to another gig or another committee or another college.

Working in the college market can be frustrating, often expensive when attending booking conferences; but once you make your way onto the scene, bookings in the college market can help fund your tour dates to less lucrative venues that build your market value. If you have an act that might play well at colleges, it just may be worth testing the waters for at least a year and see what gigs you can land to put that jingle in your pocket.

Biz Booster #98
Get Into the Minds of School Cultural Programmers

Many artists have found a welcome home in elementary schools, perhaps you are one of those artists. Booking school gigs has its own set of challenges and rewards.

Finding the right person to work with, within the school system will be different from district to district, city to city and even country to country. This is one of those situations where you need to do some research and the more locally you focus your attention at first, the more productive you'll be.

No matter who is in charge of bookings in your school or school district, a cultural arts programmer for the district, the Parent-Teacher Organization, PTO or PTA, the music teacher or the principal, the main concern is, how to relate any performance to the "Standards of Learning," in the district or "S.O.L.'s" as they are sometimes known. Relating any cultural activity to the course work is important to schools. You may have a great concert to offer, but does it teach in some way? Does it fit into any lesson plan being studied that year? Can you take your craft and turn it into a entertaining lesson that engages the students, keeps them interested while also teaches them something aligned with the dictates of learning standards demanded by the government?

Many areas have showcases for school districts or regions. Check with your school district to find out whether there is a showcase you might apply to and have an opportunity to demonstrate your programs to those who plan the school year's activities.

Timing is also a factor depending on the age group or grade level for which you are attempting to perform. Students in the lower grades have a shorter attention span so your program needs to be time-appropriate. Some school programs are offered in an assembly style situation where multiple grade levels attend at the same time. You need to plan your programs accordingly.

When planning your material, the more you can focus your approach to be both fun and educational, the more receptive the programming personnel will be. They look for acts that are colorful, present concepts that will be easily understood, think "Bill Nye, the Science Guy." If you can turn a story or a song into a participatory experience that focuses on one of the class subjects, like history, English, science, music, ecology, etc., then you have a better chance of being a hit in the schools. If you can be big and bold in your movements, colorful in your costuming, and fast paced to keep the kids actively engaged, then you may have a winning program. If you can take what you do in concert and create an experience that builds character, confidence or teaches life-learning skills in a unique way, then your services will be sought after.

If you also can provide teacher guides and classroom materials to help prepare the students for your upcoming appearance, that will help solidify your value in the school marketplace. Teachers really appreciate helpful tools to promote you and when it applies to something they are already teaching, it serves as an entertaining reinforcement of their required lessons.

Approach elementary school programmers by first, focusing their attention on what your program will teach as it relates to the sought after standards of learning. Then talk about your background and history as a performer. If you can fill a requirement with a cultural program that is not being presented currently, you will have a winner and get multiple bookings.

Taxes

Biz Booster #99
Year-End, Purchases,
Deductions & Tax Planning

November and December are perfect months to make an assessment of what supplies and tools you've got on hand to start next year and what you might need to reorder or upgrade. Look over your supplies of CDs, merchandise, promo materials, office supplies, computer hardware, software and instruments. What shape is your touring vehicle in? Does it need some repairs or new tires? Are you planning to attend any conferences or showcases next year? Perhaps you might be in time to pay early-bird-conference or showcase registrations and applications and save a bundle on those last-minute fees.

Making some much needed purchases before the end of the year may just help the deduction and depreciation pages of your tax return. If you are really on your game or have an appointment with your accountant, you may also be able to assess whether it is more tax savvy to wait to make some purchases until next year, since you may not need any more expense deductions this year.

Before the holidays capture all of your attention and you get distracted by travel and holiday parties, set aside some time during these two months to do some tax planning. Check your supplies, review your plans for the next touring season and make an appointment with your accountant to get a preliminary idea of what your tax liability will be. You'll be able to make some crucial decisions before the end of the year. This can save you money this year, or make a great start on your finances next year. You'll begin the year with the necessary tools and supplies and will have benefited from the tax deductions. For more details, check out my article: "Tax Tips for Independent Artists" (https://performingbiz.com/tax-tips-independent-artists). I know you'll find it useful.

Do you have an accountant or financial planner? Have you set up an appointment? Have you been setting aside a portion of each tour's income and making a contribution to a retirement fund? It's never too late to set one up if you haven't already.

If you've just begun touring, then there are many items that are deductible and then there are some that are not. If you're in the US, do a bit of research on the IRS website (http://www.irs.gov) to know exactly what you can include. Check publication 463, Travel, Entertainment, and Gift Expenses which details methods of deducting expenses. Look for Appendix A-1 in Publication 463, which gives you meal allowances in various cities that you can take while on business. Many cities allow larger deductions and after all, touring IS traveling for business. For other countries, check with your government's tax website for your specifics.

If you don't have an accountant yet, then this is a great time to ask some of your performer friends who they use. Look for someone who is used to working with those in the entertainment business. They may be more familiar with deductions that are specific to our industry. There's a great book you might want to check out:
The New Tax Guide for Artists of Every Persuasion by Peter J. Riley, C.P.A. (http://www.artstaxinfo.com).
Remember, a little planning now, might save you lot's of money during tax time.

Review, Replace, Refresh

Biz Booster #100
Learn from Last Year

It's so hard to get some quiet time to reflect during the holidays. Once into the start of the New Year things quiet down. In order to make the next year even better than the last one, it might be the perfect time to reflect on specific actions you took last year and see how they worked or didn't work.

Here are a few questions to help you avoid the same old problems this year and make plans for better marketing campaigns, better tours and better fan-building efforts.

What were one to three new things that you tried last year to help you book your tour dates more efficiently? How did each of them work? If they didn't work, what went wrong and how can you improve on them this year?

What were one to three new marketing strategies you used last year? Answer this question about marketing your gigs, selling your merchandise and building your fan base separately. What worked best and how can you improve on those strategies this year?

What is the one thing you wish you did last year to improve your efficiency in everything you tried? Can you do that one thing this year? Perhaps it was hiring an assistant, perhaps it was touring a new market or using a new online service to help you in specific areas of your work. Why put it off this year if it can help you be more effective and successful?

Take an hour sometime during this week to answer these questions. They may just lead to a more focused New Year, a more efficient New Year and perhaps may just re-energize your efforts for a more successful New Year.

Biz Booster Bonus Hot Tip!
Celebrate

Take a break from planning, practicing and do some partying. You've earned it after a full year of nose to the grindstone, conferences, phone calls, newsletters and emails.

I always take Christmas week and reflect, regroup, re-organize my office and get ready to dive into the New Year. It's really a great time to celebrate, but not just the holidays. It's a great time to celebrate all you've accomplished over the last year. We don't do that enough. We don't congratulate ourselves for what we've achieved, large or small.

As independent artists we are most likely not involved with an organization handing out awards at a grand ceremony. So we need to give ourselves a pat on the back and look ourselves in the mirror and simply say, "Great job!"

The fact is that no matter where you started on January 1st, you have grown in some way, you art has grown, your business has developed and you've achieved something.

So, while you are out having your holiday celebrations, don't forget to take some time to celebrate all you've accomplished last year, raise a glass of cheer and I'll do the same.

Here's to you!

Acknowledgments

My heartfelt gratitude goes out to following people for helping to make this project a reality.

Heidi Hafner, my web designer has helped make each Monday morning Biz Booster Hot Tip come to life with page design, audio players and those emergency tweaks for a quick fix before it goes live. She designs all the site upgrades and makes my crazy ideas work. I'm so grateful for her enthusiasm to work on my projects, her accessibility when I have a web issue meltdown and her techno-savvy to keep me looking good online.

Margaret Smith (Rosie) first designed my book *How To Be Your Own Booking Agent* and then all then all the updated editions. It is a joy to work with her. She has gone the extra mile and put up with my graphic quirks and sensibilities. I learn so much from her and rely on her publishing expertise during each step of this book-creation process.

Carole Ehrlich is an amazing artist whom I've known for many years and have always wanted to work with on some project. This was the time and this book cover was the project. Her expertise and complete joy in creating something I would love made this experience so fulfilling.

Irene Young has been a friend for more than thirty years. She is the artistic collaborator I turn to often and since Irene and Carole work together I am the beneficiary of incredible collaborative ideas and talent.

Lowry Olafson, singer, songwriting and consulting client spent valuable time helping me tweak the book title to find just the right words.

David Wimble, creator of *The Indie Bible* wrote and recorded the beautiful Foreword. It is entrepreneurs like David and the work he does that inspires me.

Martin Lawrie & Curfew for the use of "Future Dance" from their CD *Hold The Front Page* to open and close the audio book and for two years use as the Biz Booster Hot Tip theme music.

About the Author

Jeri Goldstein, former agent and manager, now author and music business and performing arts consultant, provides valuable resources, instruction and consulting to those navigating their way to creating a successful performing arts touring career.

How To Be Your Own Booking Agent, THE Musician's & Performing Artist's Guide To Successful Touring was self-published in 1998. The award-winning book, now in its 4th Edition, is used as a text book in Music Business courses at Universities across the U.S. and Canada and by musicians and performing artists world-wide.

Jeri presents live seminars internationally and offers tele-seminars and online courses for agents, managers, musicians and performing artists and conducts career development consultations world-wide through her Strategic Touring Career Development programs. She has transformed her live presentation to her popular online course Booking & Touring Success Strategies & Secrets which she offers twice per year. Her information-packed articles can be found on her website, https://performingbiz.com and are included in leading music business and entertainment trade magazines and on industry websites. Her free action-oriented weekly audio messages, Biz Booster Hot Tips, are designed to help musicians and performing artists make consistent progress toward reaching their career goals by offering step-by-step strategies and techniques.

Having worked with some of the top touring acoustic artists on the circuit for 20 years, she booked national and international tours for artists performing in music, theater and dance. Goldstein makes her home in Delray Beach, FL.

Goldstein has conducted seminars for:

Arts Councils:

Arts Council of the Blue Ridge
Arts Midwest
Arts North Carolina
Arts Northwest
British Columbia Touring Council, Canada
California Arts Council
Florida Department of Cultural Affairs
Indiana Arts Commission
Louisiana Division of the Arts
Mississippi Arts Commission
Missouri Folk Arts Program
New Orleans Arts Council Ohio Arts Presenter's Network
Oklahoma Arts Council Ontario Arts Council, Canada
Pennsylvania Arts Council, PennPat
Southern Arts Federation
Tennessee Arts Commission
Virginia Commission for the Arts

Schools:

Belmont University-School of Business
Carnegie Mellon University
Colorado University at Denver—Music Industry
Loyola University—Music Business Department
Music Tech College
New York University—Music Department
University of Kansas—Music & Dance Department
University of Virginia—McIntire Department of Music
University of Virginia—School of Continuing & Professional Studies

Organizations:

The Music Business Institute/ Cutting Edge
Enoch Pratt Free Library
Folk Alliance
Independent Children's Artist Network
International Bluegrass Music Association—IBMA
Louisiana Music New Orleans Pride-LMNOP
Music Entertainment Industry Educators Association—MEIEA

To order additional copies of this book, contact Performingbiz, LLC
jg@performingbiz.com   https://performingbiz.com

Get Great Gigs

Strategic Coaching for Touring Artists, Agents,
& Managers

Coaching Designed to Help You Do 3 Things:

1. Book gigs more easily

2. Get paid higher performance fees

3. Develop a loyal following to attend your shows and support your projects

Get Ready To:

- ❖ Design Your Tours to Achieve Your Goals-Artistic & Financial
- ❖ Target Your Unique Audience
- ❖ Create Audience-Specific Programs
- ❖ Match Your Marketing to Your Message
- ❖ Fully Integrate Your Personal Life with Your Artistic Career
- ❖ Recognize & Address Issues Preventing Your Success

Work with an industry professional with over 40 years of experience

- ❖ Clubs, colleges, concerts venues, festivals and niche markets
- ❖ National and international touring strategies to build profitable tours
- ❖ Resources, tools and strategies to build your career

Strategic Coaching for Touring Artists:

We assess your current situation and define a strategic plan for your future.

For information & various program details, contact Jeri Goldstein at:
https://performingbiz.com/coaching-programs
jg@performingbiz.com

www.ingramcontent.com/pod-product-compliance
Lightning Source LLC
Chambersburg PA
CBHW061045110426
42740CB00049B/2154